Disabled
Leadership

Dr. Tom A. Wiggins
Airborne Ranger (RET)

For more information,
or to contact Dr. Wiggins for book signings or
speaking events,
please visit:

https://www.facebook.com/DisabledLeadership

Disability List

Becoming Disabled (Prologue)

Chapter One: My Story: An Introduction to Disabled Leadership

Chapter Two: Self Awareness: The Strengths and Weaknesses of Disability

Chapter Three: Building Disabled Platforms

Chapter Four: Empowering Disabled Leaders

Chapter Five: The Three D's of Disabled Leadership

Chapter Six: Disabled Leaders Resilience

Chapter Seven: Share your Disability Placard

For Madeline and Gunner,
if this work inspires you,
half as much as you inspire me,
then it was worth the effort.

Disabled Leadership is a person's ability to gain self-awareness of their greatest weakness, and develop it into a platform to conceive, believe, and achieve life goals through empowerment built from a foundation of resilience.

Angel,
What's your
weakness?

Becoming Disabled
(Prologue)

Like many people, I feel like I barely managed to graduate high school. I certainly didn't stand out much academically or athletically. Out of a class of sixty-seven graduates, I succeeded in graduating somewhere in the bottom ten percent of my class. No one ever told me that there were any scholarship opportunities, or that college was even an option, that I recall. For most of my class, life would be about survival, not success, as it is with many low social economic status (SES) schools.[1] However, it was in high school that I first received what I now consider to be the finest compliment I will ever receive. "You are a leader." –Norma Wilson (Biology class)

At that point in my life, with very little experience to pull from, I did not take being called a leader as a compliment. To me, the term "leader" meant loser, it must, what had I done to be called a leader? I did not have any technical skills or special abilities. A leader is what they must call people who aren't really good at anything other than causing trouble. More importantly, I did not know how to ask for specific feedback nor did the teachers, coaches, or admin know how to provide it, which would have validated their compliment.

During and directly out of high school I worked construction where I quickly rose from laborer to mason to foreman, all under the title of leadership again. At this point I began to realize that this leadership stuff may be important. But what is leadership and why is it important?

Immediately following 9/11 I felt called to join the US Army. I enlisted and made it through Airborne and Ranger training which landed me a spot into, arguably one the world's most elite fighting forces, the 75th Ranger Regiment. I was blessed to witness, experience, and learn many different leadership styles in Regiment. It was during this time that I began informally crafting my own leadership philosophy.

In 2004 I was severely wounded during a combat operation in Afghanistan. The injuries that I sustained left me titled a "disabled veteran." Among the worst of my injuries is that I am profoundly deaf (99.237%). Little did I know, during this time of absolute confusion, what future I would have. Like many veterans in my position, I initially thought the worst: *well, I had a good run, it's over, what can I do now?* This is where I began to learn about taking opportunities and making opportunities.

Instead of moving to the beach and living comfortably on my disability pension (as I initially planned), I decided to use my disability as a platform to conceive, believe, and achieve my leadership philosophy. To do that, I needed a platform, but what?

As I medically retired from the active duty, I was recruited by Evergreen Aviation; I took the opportunity. I worked as a contract specialist for ten months while also working on a bachelor's degree full time. After ten months of dedication, I was asked to accept the responsibility of being the Executive Director of Evergreens' world class aviation museum; I made the opportunity.

During my time at Evergreen I also learned an important lesson in the meaning of failure. I was squarely behind the startup of a security company at Evergreen that would serve to support some of Evergreen's sister companies, as well other private and public sectors. There were many reasons why the company failed after a year and a half of forming. In 2008, the economy crash played a huge role, but so did poor management, lack of a shared understanding, vision, and mutual trust.

In 2009 I completed my bachelor's degree and found myself once again being recruited by the US Army; I took the opportunity. I decided to join the Army Civilian Corps and earn a master's degree. While attending the University of Kansas and working at the Command and General Staff College (CGSC) and Army Management Staff College (AMSC), I was able to build many relationships which encouraged me to stay in the area longer than originally planned and terminate my formal education with a PhD. In doing so, I have also been privileged to be surrounded by intellectual and caring senior leaders with over fifteen years of combat experience. As you will see, many of my students have also played essential roles in my leadership development.

During my time at CGSC I was an integral part of the team responsible for writing the Mid-Grade Learning Continuum for 2015, which is the common core for the Captains Career Course. Much of this curriculum is leadership driven, as Dr. John Maxwell confirms, "Everything rises and falls on leadership."[2] Upon completing the writing and piloting of the new common core, I was promoted and invited to teach leadership at the Army's premier college for civilians; the Army Management Staff College. At AMSC I am currently helping to design the Army for 2040 while teaching strategic leadership to senior level government executives.

These experiences have set the stage for this book. I hope to inspire disabled veterans and civilians alike, along with other budding leaders, to always continue to develop. True leadership never rests. I am continuously impressed by the increasing number of **D**isabled **L**eaders that come through my courses. Leadership cannot fail if development persists.

It has been my experience that disabled employees value development opportunities more than other employees. Simply considering the effort that it must have taken most folks with disabilities to get to my course alone is often humbling. Imagine if every little thing that you had to do in life, were ten times more difficult for a reason which you could not control. How would you respond? Would you give up, or would you fight through the adversity, merely to accomplish a task that may be simple to an ordinary person? What is an ordinary person?

The previous two sentences provide alternative perspectives. Perspective one, an ordinary person is better than a disabled person. Perspective two, an ordinary person isn't better than anyone. Let's change the noun. Instead of ordinary person, what about ordinary leader? Is an ordinary leader better than a disabled leader? Would you want to grow your organization with ordinary leaders? I think that there is some value there, but that probably would not be my focus. Now, for the difficult question: would you want to grow your organization with Disabled Leaders? If you're scratching your head, that's understandable. In this book I want to introduce you to what a Disabled Leader is, and more importantly, what a Disabled Leader can be.

As you will hopefully come to appreciate, you do not have to be disabled person to be a Disabled Leader. Disabled Leaders set many wonderful examples for us on a daily basis which we can use to influence and inspire others the way that they have us. By changing the way, we consider daily opportunities and adversity, we earn the ability to improve not only ourselves, but also our organizations.

My last thoughts before we jump into the contents and concepts of this book, are on the potential demographics of my readers. As I am writing this, I envision what it might look like sitting on the shelf in the store or library. In my mind, seventy-five percent of potential readers picked up this book because of the graphic on the cover. Perhaps the reader has a disability herself or knows someone with a disability. These people might be looking for some inspiration. Then there is the other twenty-five percent. For these readers, the title grabbed their attention more than the illustration. These readers might be more cynical. They have experienced toxic leadership, bad bosses, and terrible organizations. This demographic is looking for ways to influence their experiences, operational environment, and colleagues. I am writing this book for both groups. I hope that everyone finds something that they need, and more importantly, that they can use. Leadership, for me, is the

ability to inspire and influence others; and that is my goal
here.

My Story
An Introduction to Disabled Leadership

I walked into the gym, if for nothing more than to shake off the winter chill, in its musky warmth. I had been a POWR (Prisoner of Walter Reed Army Medical Center) for a year and a half, and it was beginning to show on my waist line as well as my mental wellness. I expected the building to be empty and unused. Most of us wounded warriors despised physical therapy, and the thought of conducting personal PT, in my condition, on top of rehabilitation, exhausted me. What started as a pretty darn good excuse had become an unacceptable expectation of helplessness. "How did I get here?" I'd often ask myself.

A year and a half earlier I endured a four-hour fire fight on the Afghanistan and Pakistan border. I was on a four-man observation point (OP) that partially served to protect a Ranger blocking position (BP) five hundred feet down the mountain. We caught Taliban forces attempting to set up an early morning ambush about two hours before dawn. What we didn't know, is that so had the other OPs. The enemy was staging a complete 360-degree ambush, and if they had they succeeded, it would have been a massacre.

Despite the appearance of our bunker and surrounding area following the fight, no Ranger was seriously injured in the battle. Several vehicles had been destroyed by RPGs (Rocker Propelled Grenades) and a couple of Rangers had minor wounds and injuries. Incredibly, the four of us on OP "Club One," had thrown all of our grenades, we had two magazines of ammunition left between the four of us, and a Gustav round had been shot, but not exploded less than four feet from our faces. We lasted until sunrise when air support scared off the last of the combatants.

As a twenty-one-year-old Ranger, who had already survived five combat deployments, and now the most intense fire fight of my enlistment, I felt invincible. If I wasn't certain before, I was now, we could not die. We were too good to be bested by our enemies. In this country, we felt as though we were gods amongst men. All of the variables were there for what would happen next; cockiness and complacency, certainly a recipe for disaster, a lesson I was soon to learn.

A week later, we had broken down the BP, because the enemy obviously knew we were there and was avoiding us. Command decided that is was time to move to our next location. We spent the day breaking down the BP and OPs, and loading vehicles. If the enemy was watching, it was obvious that we would be moving soon. We left immediately after dark. It was a moonless night which made the movement slow. Even with night vision, it was nearly impossible to see. From my position, as top gunner, all I could see was a line of IR Chemlights (these could only be seen with night vision goggles). If I couldn't see anything, then the enemy surely couldn't, right? It was going to be a long boring night movement, nothing like the battle from a week before, which still coursed my veins. My mind wandered as I halfheartedly scanned the ridgeline.

Of course, I was not the only one with these thoughts and feelings. Many others must have been bored, tired, and distracted as we crept along the valley. One of the last things I would ever hear with my God given sense, was a conversation below me on the Gun Mounted Vehicle (GMV). The clear violation of noise discipline proved far less costly than the violation of light discipline, as the vehicle commander opened his laptop. The enemy didn't need night vision goggles to see the colorful screen light up the inside of my GMV.

Seconds after his serious mistake of opening the laptop, an RPG slammed into the top of the vehicle. The RPG slammed into me. For a second, just a second, I heard muffled screaming. They were yelling my name: Wiggins, Wiggins, Wiggi...Then the sound became as dark as the night. I died.

Worse than my death, my Ranger buddies were seriously injured. One of my best friends had his arms snapped in half by an RPG. Another Ranger lost his eye. I think, worse than the physical injuries, they were both conscious for the entire fire fight. They endured the suffering, the pain, the unknown of what was happening or what would happen. As I died, they were still screaming my name.

I have no memory of the fire fight that ensued. I have no recollection of my friends crying in pain and fear. I never saw my killer's face. I don't recall dying three times on a foreign battlefield. What I do remember, is that I am "immortal", and that played a role in this tragedy. Our cockiness and complacency let the enemy prevail that night and forever changed the lives of a handful of patriots.

Now, a year and a half into my recovery, the cockiness was gone, but complacency was worse than ever. I was a severely injured combat veteran, that is what it was, and what it would be, I had accepted it for what it was. I suffered from a severe traumatic brain injury which left me deaf and constantly disoriented. My back looks like swiss cheese and is filled with shrapnel. Recovery was a long process. I had learned how to do a lot of things again during the past year. I was walking pretty good. I could even get into a pool without immediately drowning. For a Ranger who was used to twenty-mile road marches and seventy-five-meter swim tests, I was devastated. The thought of going to a hospital gym seemed futile, but there I stood.

I was surprised to see some of the soldiers I had met in physical therapy (PT), working out in the gym. In PT, they seemed as disenfranchised as me. Now, here I stood, in the entrance of the small weight room, watching a half a dozen wounded warriors pushing themselves to recovery. It was impressive. Joe, whom I had talked to many times in PT, was doing pull ups. Joe had lost all of his limbs except for one arm. He was doing one armed pull ups! Everywhere I looked, wounded warriors pulling themselves out of wheelchairs, and onto fitness machines. I felt two things: First, I felt ashamed. I was a Ranger, I was supposed to be better than these "common soldiers", but they were embarrassing me. Secondly, I felt inspired. If Joe could do one armed pull ups, there was no excuse for me not to be doing something, or anything.

Although to this day, I still cannot complete a one-armed pullup, the experience still inspires me. These soldiers were disabled. Some may not have had high expectations of them, but they had formidable expectations of themselves. When I am lacking desire, determination, or dedication I revisit that weight room, because they introduced me to the power of Disabled Leadership.

In this book, I want to examine the power in the concept of Disabled Leadership. Why do some rise to the occasion, annihilate obstacles, and achieve greatness while others accept defeat or minimum expectations? How can disabled leaders emulate the traits desire, determination, and dedication that Disabled Leaders leverage? What is a Disabled Leader?

You probably noticed in the previous paragraph that I identified two types of leaders: disabled leaders with a lower-case d, and Disabled Leaders, with a capital D. As you will read, the difference in the two is enormous. Disabled Leaders, with a capital D, have experienced something in life which has, or attempted to, handicap them in some way. disabled leaders, with a lowercase d, tend to create handicaps for themselves, their colleagues and employees, and their organization. Disabled Leaders, with a capital D, face challenges head on despite inconveniences and setbacks. disabled leaders, with a lowercase d, have excuses and explanations for every encounter. While I find Disabled Leaders far more inspiring, disabled leaders can also prove interesting to analyze in an effort to develop them into Disabled Leaders.

I understand that using the terms Disabled/disabled Leader in different contexts may prove confusing to readers, or difficult to keep up with, to assume the least. In an effort to remind you, of the difference between the two terms I have highlighted each term differently. In addition to capitalizing **D**isabled **L**eadership, I have also bolded the **D.** When you see the bold capital **D**, you should remember, this is what we are trying to achieve. When you see the lowercased d, underlined as such, that is a reminder that the trait or behavior is something that we should develop. Once we understand this, we can all achieve **D**isabled **L**eadership.

In this book, we will attempt to compare and contrast how these two types of leaders might approach leadership opportunities and challenges differently. As you have undoubtedly noticed by this point, I consider **D**isabled **L**eaders to be a substantial strength, and I encourage adding this diversity to any organizational portfolio. However, disabled leaders will typically prove to be a considerable liability for any organization or business. We must learn how to properly develop disabled leaders, and help them understand how to improve themselves, their leadership, and their organizations.

My primary disability is deafness, and that is how I came up with the concept of **D**isabled **L**eadership. I am deaf, with a lower-case d. Although I have grown an appreciation for Deaf culture, with a capital D, I am not a part of it. Deaf culture requires more than deafness and awareness. At a minimum, Deaf culture requires fluency in American Sign Language (ASL), and many Deaf people are actively involved in the Deaf community. Likewise, **D**isabled **L**eadership requires more than awareness of leadership skills. It requires fluency in the leadership, and commitment to mastering various leadership traits, which will be introduced and discussed in this book.

Deaf culture does not require that you be born deaf, or deaf at all to join their community. Many people, like myself, become deaf later in life. However, the earlier you become Deaf, the easier it is to fit in to the Deaf community. I have been deaf for fifteen years, and I am astutely aware of the Deaf community, yet I have not joined it. The Deaf community does not judge me for not immersing myself into their culture. I have read books, I am aware of their history, and customs, but I have been unable or unwilling to master ASL.

Like Deaf culture, Disabled Leadership also attracts, encourages, and accepts new members into its community. However, Disabled Leadership may be a bit more unforgiving. You can't just read about it and accept its presence; you must live to improve your leadership every day. disabled leadership, in a sense, is unacceptable to Disabled Leaders.

I am currently a Professor of Strategic Leadership at Army University. In these leadership courses we primarily serve Department of Defense executives. That is about where the similarities end. By design, the classes are diversified as much as you could expect. I have seasoned students with decades of experience learning alongside of students fresh out of high school and college. I recently had a 93-year-old WWII veteran, Fred Chapel, take my course. I can only imagine what Fred was thinking that first hour of class. I looked Fred straight in the eye and asked him if that eighteen-year-old girl can be a leader. Of course she can, that's why she is here.

The beauty of leadership is that anyone can be a leader, just as anyone can be a Disabled Leader. This can be difficult for many people to accept so let me say it again; ANYONE can be a Leader. One might argue that this has not always been the case. During the industrial age, many workers did not view themselves as leaders upon entering the work force.[3] They were taught that leadership was a position, and that if they came in early and worked late then one day, far from now, they could possibly be a leader. Today's emerging leaders do not believe that to be entirely accurate. The information age has changed the conditions, and environment in which workers think and operate. Leaders can be found anywhere of any age. Great examples of young leaders include Mark Zuckerburg the founder of FaceBook and Charlene Begley CIO of General Electric; both have proven themselves to be terrific leaders who defy industrial era leadership logic. However, we must remember that leadership is not a position, it is a process.

I am willing to guess that you have probably heard of at least one of those two previous young leaders that I mentioned. However, the title of this work isn't Young Leaders, it is **D**isabled **L**eadership. So, I ask you this, can you think of any **D**isabled **L**eaders? If you were able to think of one or more, is that **D**isabled **L**eader famous? Is it obvious that this **D**isabled **L**eader is disabled? A couple of modern **D**isabled **L**eaders who come to mind might be President Franklin D. Roosevelt or Professor Stephen Hawking. These **D**isabled **L**eaders are easy to notice and serve as icons to other **D**isabled **L**eaders. You might be surprised how many other leaders you know that are **D**isabled **L**eaders. For fun, make a list of ten leaders whom have inspired you. Now go research them and see how many have faced a disability. You might be surprised. One of my personal favorites is Lou Ferrigno, who is 80% deaf; HULK SMASH![4] By the end of this book, I hope that you will be inspired by how many **D**isabled **L**eaders you interact with on a daily basis.

Some baby boomers reading this are ready to throw the book away already. Let me assure you that, although I am identified as Generation Y, I am more Generation X than millennial. Some people are now referring to that as Xennial.[5] I point this out because it could be easy to think my understanding and approach to leadership is a product of the "everyone gets a trophy" culture that is prevalent in our society.[6] I get the skepticism; I do. How can EVERYONE be a leader? Who would follow? I hear it from students every class. "I'm not a leader. I'm not in a leadership position. I'm not a supervisor." All great excuses, and all wrong.

We have all been guilty of referring to management as leadership no matter what our views are of them. It is common to hear, in any organization, that leadership is horrible or has failed in some way. Well, if that is the case, then are they really leading you? Why?

One of the most important concepts that I try to help leaders in my classes understand, is the difference between management and leadership. Management is a position or a task. Leadership is a process. The process that makes a leader is not standardized. Because everyone leads a little differently, the process will always vary, at least slightly. Call me biased, but I have bought into the US Army's old definition of leadership, at least partially. Leadership is the ability to influence and inspire others while accomplishing the mission and improving the organization. Suddenly the light bulb comes on. The part that resounds with most people is the part which I embrace: the ability to influence and inspire. If I were a betting man, I would guess that you have influenced someone along the way. Even if you can't think of how or when, it has surely happened. Once we can begin to break down the concept of leadership in this manner, it becomes much easier to understand and accept. I make automatic assumptions that my students typically "accomplish the mission" or they would likely be in the unemployment line, and not my leadership class. Lastly, simply by attending a leadership seminar (or reading this book) I can argue that you are improving yourself and your organization. It just makes sense, but don't take my word for it, pause here and think back to a time when you were influential or influenced. How did it happen? Was it intentional? Were you aware that you were being influential?

Now, think back to 93-year-old Fred, and his 18-year-old classmate. If old people can be leaders, and young people can be leaders then it stands to reason that disabled people can be leaders too; and they are usually some of the best. Persons with disabilities make good leaders because they tend to be empathetic, inspiring, innovative, and hard workers. What are some other attributes that you might add to this list? Empathy is an essential leadership trait for **D**isabled **L**eaders. If a leader cannot put himself in another's shoes, then he will not be able to understand when and why challenges arise. Consider a personal or professional experience that could have been more positive or developmental if someone would have tried to understand your perspective or position. If a person cannot identify with another or identify challenges then she will have a rough time being an effective leader; in fact, one could say she is a disabled leader.

Please do not set this book aside just because you are not disabled yourself. There is something for you in this book, I guarantee it. If you cannot understand or are not buying that anyone can be a **D**isabled **L**eader because you don't perceive most people as disabled, please allow me to dispel that notion. I offer that every person that I have ever met has been disabled at some time or another during their life. Try not to be too offended.

We have all been disabled at one point or another in our lives. Many of us are disabled right now and do not even know it. We share a common disability. This disability is far more crippling than losing legs, vision, or hearing. We let this thing cripple us, and we limp through life believing that it is just something that we must live with. The good news is that we have the power to end it. Like many physical and mental handicaps, we have the ability to improve or overcome this disability. The most common disability, that has affected every person on this planet at some point, is *fear*.

Fear is what keeps most people from achieving their potential. A doctor tells a patient he will never walk again, the patient tries to stand up but falls down; the fear becomes real. A student fails a pop quiz, and now thinks that college is too hard, and drops out; the fear becomes real. An entrepreneur is told repeatedly that his good idea isn't financially feasible; the fear becomes real. We handicap ourselves based on other people's expectations and other peoples fear by making it our own.[7] What about the patient who falls down but gets back up again and again, until six months later he can stand on his own? The student who sticks out the difficult coursework and ends up going to grad school? The entrepreneur that founded the Fortune 100 company? The guy who quit? Who gets respected and remembered? **D**isabled **L**eadership strives to overcome fear.

Fear is such a broad concept. When I ask you to overcome your fear, I don't necessarily mean that if you are afraid of great white shark, then go swim with one; let's be reasonable. Maybe start with a bull shark. Just kidding, don't do that. Seriously though, start small. Small victories will build confidence to fight fear.[8] If you are afraid of public speaking, then start with a small audience you trust. This will allow you to develop experience, improve techniques, and build confidence. Soon you will be comfortable with speaking in other environments with other people. You may be surprised to find yourself overcoming your fear.

I have asked thousands of executives what their biggest fear is. Overwhelmingly, the top two responses that I receive are Public Speaking and Failure. Why are those things to be afraid of? We live in a culture that glorifies public speaking, i.e. actors, politicians, sports, everyone has a public opinion, so why is it scary? We live in a culture of bankruptcy and public welfare so why is everyone so scared of failure? The truth is, we are not scared of either of those things, we are afraid of judgement. How will we be judged if we screw up what we are trying to convey or look silly? We may be judged as a failure if we fail. The question really evolves to, why do we fear judgement?

Fear, in the context of judgement, is better known as social anxiety.[9] Social anxiety is a theory that captures just about anything and everything we could possibly be judged by, especially in a professional setting. This is the reason so many agencies and corporations have leadership training, to help overcome social difficulties. Most people do not have issues with the technical aspect of their jobs, but with the social aspect; dealing with other people. Addressing and practicing their weaknesses in a safe environment allows movement. If we don't trust those whom we work and live with enough to leave our comfort zone, then how can we do it in training with a bunch of strangers? Training forces students out of their comfort zone while family and friends encourage us to be just as comfortable as possible. Also, if it is too horrible, at least I won't have to see most of these people ever again after the training. These excuses get us started.

I'm mentioning this because I have noticed an unfair amount of cynicism regarding the effectiveness of leadership training. Typically, the skepticism is from people who have never been to a leadership course. Many have never been selected, they form a resentment to those whom have, and what they got from the class. Most of these people learn that they were not selected due to their own lack of initiative; simply asking. Of course, some people have had bad training experiences. Perhaps the instructors weren't very good, or there was mismanaged conflict in the class. I often find that most people get out of the course what they put into it, more than how others influence it.

There are a lot of very experienced leadership facilitators out there. The trick is finding the ones who are trying to learn as much as the class itself. The leadership awareness and techniques picked up in training can push Disabled Leaders into new stratospheres. Leadership training should not be viewed by management or employees as a distraction or liability. Good leadership training will reap undreamt rewards. If possible, work with a program that will tailor to your organization's needs. Ask questions and your trainer should have quite a few questions for you before the program starts as well. Invest time in selecting the right course or speaker for you, and you will notice immediate improvement within your organization. Ok, I have procrastinated for as long as I can. That concludes this side bar. Now, let me tell you about my fear.

I want to open this book by being as painfully transparent with you as possible. I hope this will allow you to be honest with yourself, and with me. My biggest fear is *being forgotten*, and it disables me at times. Less than ten years after being severely wounded, I felt that the Army and the country had forgotten my service and sacrifice; so, I came back into the Army, to validate my convictions and service. My children have been kidnapped, as the result of an ugly divorce that has relocated them two thousand miles away from me, and I worry they will forget me; so, when I get to see them, I am a "Disneyland Dad," attempting to fabricate as many memories as possible in a short amount of time. I spend so much time wondering who will remember me after I leave this earth that it impacts my present, and possibly future. My fear is one reason I want to be a writer. I secretly hope that one day I will write something that will last long after I am gone; and therefor, people will remember me.

My fear is being forgotten, but my disability is failing to accept what is and live in the present. Fear is a disability. Given greater context, I actually leverage, perhaps a healthy level of fear, in order to achieve a goal, becoming a writer. The trick is figuring out how to use the fear, and not letting the fear use you. As we work through this book, perhaps we will uncover an underlying issue that you are currently unaware of, something which is disabling you. It will be up to you to decide what to do with what you learn.

Just as if you were in my classroom, consider this book your safe place. Some concepts may make you uncomfortable, and that is ok. I am going to ask you repeatedly to leave your comfort zone. That does not just refer to the things that scare you, but also the ideas you believe are wrong or silly. Just give every concept fair consideration, no matter how senseless it seems. Give it a try, you might be surprised what works for you.

I have organized this book by deconstructing what I believe makes a **D**isabled **L**eader so valuable, and disabled leaders so costly. Each chapter will examine how to leverage **D**isabled **L**eader's capabilities, and how to develop disabled leaders' shortcomings. It is my hope to not only create awareness and understanding for these leaders, but also their organizations.

Awareness is a smart place to start understanding what, how, and why we lead. So, that is where we will begin our journey in the next chapter. Once we are able to grasp understanding of our strengths and weaknesses, and figure out how to leverage and develop them, then we should be able to build a foundation that will allow our leadership to grow. The first step to **D**isabled **L**eadership is self-awareness.

Self-Awareness: The Strengths and Weaknesses of

Disability

While earning my bachelor's degree I was enrolled
in several courses with an accounting major name
Stephanie. During our first course together, I barely
noticed Stephanie because I always sat in the front of the
class, and she always sat in the back of the room near the
exit. The course was primarily lecture with minimal
discussion, and no group work. I sat in the front of the
class in order to be able to hear better and read lips, and I
would find out later that Stephanie sat near the exit
because she was blind and would simply choose the first
seat that she could find.

I found myself enrolled in several more courses
with Stephanie over the years and was always amazed by
the circumstances. What are the odds that a deaf guy and
a blind girl would be enrolled in the same courses at a
small liberal arts college? What events must have
unfolded for that to be?

Stephanie was born blind and certainly faced a
different set of challenges than me; I was rendered deaf at

age twenty-one. Over the course of eighteen years Stephanie was able to embrace her capabilities and accept her limitations as nothing more than mere challenges that she could overcome. If no one ever expected me to go to college before I became deaf, then they certainly wouldn't after. However, we were both able to find our starting point somewhere in our disability.

Stephanie was raised with people, mostly outside of her family, constantly doubting her ability to accomplish even a high school diploma. She now holds a bachelor's degree from a prestigious undergraduate university, and the last time I spoke with her, she was enrolled in graduate school. These situations do not only apply to academia and employment, but also extra curricula activities. Stephanie also ran hurdles on the track and field team in high school. I recommend going to your local or state school for the blind, and picking up a track and field schedule, then be prepared to be amazed! My experience with Stephanie was the first time I really began considering the value the Disabled Leaders add value to organizations. Simply put, Stephanie inspired me.

Although Stephanie did have some negative energy surrounding her development, she also had a good deal of support. Stephanie attributes much of her success to her family and friends. These folks instilled an expectation of hard work, and showed Stephanie that opportunities existed. If Stephanie had been smothered with sympathy instead of support, how successful do you think she would be? Consider how many times or circumstances in which you simply did something for someone instead of helping them develop. How long until that behavior becomes an expectation?[10] While this type of assistance may be helpful to the individual, and perhaps even yourself in the short run, in the grand scheme it does nothing to develop the person or the organization. Stephanie's support team understood the value of development. With this knowledge and desire Stephanie was prepared for a healthy dose of self-awareness.

When Disabled Leaders hear the term self-awareness, they most likely start considering their capabilities and limitations. This is as good of a place as any to start. The best way to go about this task is to consider capabilities and limitations separately. It can be hard enough to distinguish the two at times, because we often lack the self-awareness required, and this should make the process a little easier. Afterall, self-awareness is the point of this exercise.

Begin by identifying relevant capabilities. If you are a contract specialist, then the number of free throws that you can make with a basketball may be irrelevant. Try to identify at least five supporting actions such as: great typist, multi-tasker, committed, critical thinker, and effective communicator. If you are having difficulties coming up with five capabilities, then you can either leave the list short for now or attempt to be even vaguer. I find value in beginning broadly, and then narrowing things down to be as precise as possible. Cast your net to grab as much as possible, and then cinch it down to see what substance you find. Once you have this list, set it aside, and then do the same thing for your list of limitations. Do not look back at your capabilities list until you have completed the second list as to not risk cross contamination. My list of limitations include: hearing, prioritizing, time management, experience, and focus.

These potential shortcomings may limit my ability to effectively lead.

Now, compare the two side by side. Do any of the functions on the separate lists conflict with each other? For example, I have effective communicator listed as a strength, but I also have hearing listed as a limitation. Isn't active listening important for effective communication?[11] This may be worth a second look. Another issue to look for is whether items on one list are causing items on the other. I have multi-tasker as capability and focus as a limitation. My multi-tasking may be rendering me unable to focus adequately on some things. Make a third list containing the items that conflict or are obviously connected, such as my examples.

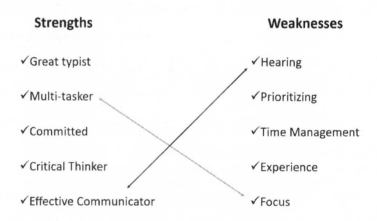

Strengths	Weaknesses
✓Great typist	✓Hearing
✓Multi-tasker	✓Prioritizing
✓Committed	✓Time Management
✓Critical Thinker	✓Experience
✓Effective Communicator	✓Focus

Now that we have self-identified, what we perceive to be, our top five capabilities and our top five limitations lets expand our lists even further. For each action on the list write down three specific examples or experiences that lead you to believe that the action is a capability or a limitation. This should be a fairly easy task. If you absolutely cannot come up with any examples, then consider removing that action from its respected list and replacing it. By making the lists more specific you are validating your beliefs. For example, I believe that my hearing is a limitation because I don't take phone calls, sometimes I make guesses at what a person just said, and it is easier for me to space out.

The last step that I recommend is to show your lists to someone that you trust. Consider a mentor, spouse, or a friend. Ask this person to provide honest feedback on your lists. You can still take or leave what you like, but this should provide you with an alternative perspective. Now you can reflect on how you perceive yourself, and how others perceive you.

Understanding your capabilities and limitations, as a **D**isabled **Le**ader, provides a clear first step into self-awareness. Realizing your capabilities allows you the opportunity to build on these traits, and perfect skills. Considering your limitations helps to identify areas of improvement. Just because you perceive yourself to have a limitation does not mean that you lack the ability to develop that skill. In fact, I will argue that once you have identified your limitations you should immediately begin considering ways to develop them into strengths. For **D**isabled **L**eaders, leveraging is more useful than mitigating. Likewise, this is not a one and done deal. Once you feel as though you have improved your capabilities, and have also at least acknowledged your limitations, you will be on your way to self-awareness.

I have told you that you should figure out how to develop your weaknesses. That is easy for me to say but may not be so easy for you to do. Often disabled leaders will simply sweep their weaknesses under the rug, and attempt to ignore them. disabled leaders may become quite good at ignoring their weaknesses, however glaring they may become, but inevitably they will prove to be an issue for colleagues and employees. In turn these weaknesses will rear their ugly heads for the disabled leader.

The question then becomes, how can we develop our weaknesses, and avoid becoming a disabled leader? Unfortunately, there is no simple answer or magic solution. There is no easy fix. Developing weaknesses takes dedication and patience. Looking back at my list of weaknesses I have chosen to work on my focus.

Focus is one of my perceived weaknesses which I have validated by providing examples of how I lose focus, and thereby productivity and effectiveness. I have also realized that I listed multi-tasking a strength, and I have recognized that there may be a connection here. The first thing that I want to do is spend some time reflecting the potential gains and losses of attempting to change these processes. Is it worth being more focused and thereby effective, to reduce my strength in multi-tasking which may cause me to lose productivity? Am I losing productivity by having to redo tasks because I am multi-tasking, and not focused? Start asking yourself the hard questions, challenge your preconceptions. Don't just think about them, write them down, and make your ideas tangible. More importantly than asking yourself the hard questions is make sure that you at least attempt to answer them.

For my exercise, the answer is yes, the benefit of being more focused is worth the cost limiting my perceived strength, multi-tasking. In my reflection, I came to understand, that for me, greater focus would help me to be more efficient than multi-tasking.[12] I would prefer to do one thing right the first time than do five things and have to fix three of them. During my reflection, I realized that my perception had changed over time. I used to prefer to get as much done as quickly as possible, and if I needed to adjust, or fix things later, I could. Time and experience change our perspective, and it is a continuously evolving process. As I have stated, this is not a one and done deal, but an on-going process.

Now that I am certain that I want to be more focused, I must figure out how. The how to change in this case, and in most cases, is behavioral. For example, if I know that I need to focus on a project today, how can I limit distractions? Maybe instead of leaving my outlook email up all day I will set aside a few times during the day which I can check email, and the rest of the day stay offline. This can help limit thinking about other due outs, and happenings around the office. As hard as it may be to fathom, maybe I could even log off of social media for the day! Undoubtedly, especially at first, I will be tempted just to make sure that the boss hasn't sent an important email or that my spouse's luncheon went well. The only person that can change you is you.

It will be hard. Maintaining focus by cutting communication may seem excessive to some leaders. After all, most leaders agree that communication is foundational to leadership.[13] Each change will be situational and call for different sacrifices. The sacrifices do not have to be permanent, but must last long enough to spur the desired change. You should also consider warning those affected by the change. For example, if I know that I want to focus on a project this week and only intend to check my email twice per day, then I might set up an out of office message explaining the situation. Even if the change you seek causes a short-term negative impact in your life or organization, you should remember the long-term benefit of this change.

What if you have a weakness that you cannot change or develop? First of all, ask yourself, why can't I change or develop this weakness? Make sure that you are not being a disabled leader. disabled leaders make excuses. Disabled Leaders find a way. If you cannot figure out how to develop your weakness, then you must consider how to mitigate the way the weakness is causing you to be a disabled leader.

Let's think about Stephanie again for a minute. Stephanie has just listed her weaknesses, and like a good Disabled Leader, she was transparently honest with herself. The very first item in her weakness column is blindness. Although there is expensive medical technology that may help Stephanie, let's assume that she cannot improve her sight. Stephanie is a Disabled Leader, so she knows that she must mitigate her weakness in order to be successful. Remember how she chose the seat closest to the classroom door? She was diminishing the probability that she would trip over a desk, a back pack, or another student.

Stephanie also ran the 400m hurdles in high school. That doesn't sound like she was mitigating her weakness or risk! Stephanie knew that she had a weakness that she couldn't change, but she was still willing to challenge herself. I am certain that Stephanie didn't just wake up one day, go to the track, and run 400m. She probably walked that track a thousand times. She likely stepped on and over the hurdles, gauging the height and ability required and the number of steps between each hurdle, even more times than she walked the track. Disabled Leaders commit and dedicate themselves to their goals, and their organizational goals. disabled leaders can develop and challenge themselves just like Disabled Leaders. It starts with self-awareness and develops with commitment. By the way, I got to see Stephanie run a race at the college level, and she placed third.

Disabled Leaders should realize that self-awareness is more than merely capabilities and limitations. We need to consider our behaviors and emotions. I think that we understand, by this point, that our capabilities are a direct reflection of our behaviors. I ask you to also consider how your behaviors are driven by your emotions. By understanding how we feel, we can modify the way we act. If I am frustrated it may be difficult for me to get excited about a task. The emotion may inhibit understanding or motivation for the purpose. By acknowledging the emotion, it becomes easier to modify the behavior to something more productive.

As we continue to consider the importance of empathy, emotions can serve as strong clues for behavior. If a teammate appears distracted and anxious, and is being unproductive, we can make a safe assumption that there is a correlation. From there, the leader can make decisions for how to handle the situation much easier. Displaying empathy may gain greater influence with the teammate. If you present the problem to her in an understanding and empathetic manner, you potentially have a better chance of influencing the scenario. This considerate approach will help the teammate become aware of her perceived attitude and behaviors. It will be far easier to shift gears when the feedback is provided in a transformative manner rather than authoritative. By helping her be successful you are also helping yourself, and your entire team be successful.

Self-Assessment

Strengths: 1._____

                      2._____

                      3._____

                      4._____

                      5._____

Validation: 1._____

                      2._____

                      3._____

                      4._____

                      5._____

Weaknesses: 1._____

                      2._____

                      3._____

                      4._____

                      5._____

Correlations: 1._____

                      2._____

                      3._____

disabled leaders maintain weaknesses and Disabled Leaders build strengths

When I was Executive Director of Evergreen Aviation Museum (EAM) campus, I learned a lot about building teams. We had an interesting mix of dynamics. First was the sheer size. Our paid staff was only around fifty employees, but our volunteer staff was over three hundred strong. Different and often conflicting policies between the two staffs created unique challenges. For example, I once had to fire a paid employee for taking a free lunch from the café. She had seen a volunteer do this the day before and assumed that it was allowed (that was her alibi.) Yes, it was allowed for our volunteer staff, but not for the paid staff. This was the same week that she was reprimanded for taking excessive smoke breaks because she'd seen volunteers doing that as well. There is more to this story, but you get the point, that there were big differences in the way the teams could operate.

Our volunteer staff consisted primarily of Vietnam veterans. The average age of our volunteers was somewhere around 65, right around retirement age. The range was broader. We had WWII vets and Iraq vets.

These veterans brought with them a wide range of knowledge, skills, and abilities. It was our challenge to find the best fit for them in the museum. Some were more obvious than others. If a volunteer was a B29 bomber pilot, it made sense to assign him to that wing of the museum. By doing so he could share his vast knowledge, and first-hand experiences with the airplane. You can't buy that type of storyboard.

However, if we had a volunteer who was a finance officer in the Army, as much as we may have wanted to, we couldn't put him in the accounting office. These volunteers did everything from lead tours, restore airplanes, and even act as a door greeter. Regardless of their previous military station or rank, they humbly accepted these positions out of passion to educate and inspire.

Sometimes it is easy to leverage strengths. It's easy to match a pilot to his airplane. Other times, building a team may take a little more thought, and a lot more work. Even if you get a perfect resume hire there is no guarantee that he will be a perfect fit for a given position. It is nearly impossible to accurately gauge, in an interview, how a new personality will interact with the current team dynamics. For example, the new teammate may overplay a strength (I have an MBA and therefor I know the *right way* to do everything) or have a glaring weakness (I am terrible at public speaking). A d̲isabled l̲eader may be tempted to quickly terminate the new teammate and rid himself of the perceived liability. A **D**isabled **L**eader understands the challenges and opportunities that a new team dynamic offer.

At Evergreen Aviation Museum we were honored to house many special aircraft. This, of course, included Howard Hughes' world famous Spruce Goose. Under the wings of the Spruce Goose sit well over one hundred historical aircraft, many of which served in combat. Of these fine machines, EAM displayed a storied P-51 Mustang. The Mustang had been fully restored and was even airworthy. Occasionally, for special events, EAM would let her fly to joy of all who were present. Needless to say, we were quite proud to have her in our collection.

One day, I had the pleasure of sitting in on a volunteer interview with the day captain. (Of course, the volunteers implemented a chain of command!) The prospective volunteer was a WWII and Korean veteran pilot named Rusty. When I was told that he was a P-51 pilot, I knew it was an interview that I couldn't miss. Boy was I right! He had amazing stories and knew everything about the aircraft. The day captain and I knew immediately that this young pilot (80+years old) would be a treasure for the community. We were able to schedule Rusty to volunteer on Saturdays, which was generally our busiest day of the week.

I would often volunteer at the museum on the weekends too; either Saturday or Sunday, but rarely both. As luck would have it, I was there for our new star P-51 pilot's first day. Everyone introduced themselves to Rusty and shook his hand before the museum opened. I have always been amazed at how veterans can immediately become old friends. Just before we opened the doors that day, the day captain and I walked Rusty to the Mustang and showed him a sign that we had made introducing him as an authentic P-51 Mustang pilot. Rusty sat down at the small desk which was provided and smiled approvingly.

Just before noon the day captain waved me over to speak with him. Apparently, there had already been a few complaints about our new P-51 pilot. Complaints included foul language, and inappropriate behavior towards children. The day captain was quite concerned; as was I. Contrary to popular belief, just like volunteers are hired, they can be fired. The day captain's indication was that we intended to do just that. I was able to encourage him to let Rusty finish the day, and then we could both talk with him.

Before the day was out there was in fact another incident where the pilot smacked a child's hand while touching the Mustang; touching aircrafts was against the rules. Something had to be done. I couldn't allow this sort of behavior to continue, but I knew that Rusty was something special to the museum and I wanted to do everything that I could to make it work.

As you might imagine, when the museum closed at 5p.m., some of the older volunteers begin to get a little grumpy. Rusty was no exception. The day captain and I approached the pilot and asked if we might speak with him to which we were promptly told "not today, I'm tired." The day captain was visibly irritated and ready to excuse Rusty from his position. I replied to the volunteer

"I understand, but we will need to speak before you are able to volunteer anymore." The old timer glared at me and then matter-of-factly stated "ok, I quit." I was floored as I watched this hero hand the day captain his vest and take his leave.

That evening, well after dinner, I was still bothered by the day's incident. Upon reflecting on the day's events, and my previous encounter with the volunteer, it just wasn't adding up. At his interview, he seemed to be a pleasant and caring individual who shared the same values as the museum and was motivated to educate and inspire our visitors. This morning, he was friendly with all the other volunteers. It seemed to be the guests that were causing him issue. However, in his interview he mentioned that he loved meeting new people and sharing his stories. None of this was making sense to me, but I was determined to figure it out. I resolved that on Monday I would try to make contact and find an opportunity to talk with him.

I've shared this story in the past and some folks think that I am crazy. I was the Executive Director of a rapidly expanding museum campus. I had enough actual paid employee problems to fill my days without looking for more. I have already admitted that we had over three hundred volunteers, so it is not as though we were short staffed. Why waste my time with one volunteer?

I've alluded to it several times already, and now I will outright say it: **D**isabled **L**eaders care. Whereas it would be easy for a disabled leader to fire and forget a day one volunteer, the **D**isabled **L**eader will struggle with where she went wrong and what she could do to help the situation. **D**isabled **L**eaders understand that not all problems may be readily visible. Sometimes, what may seem to be a clear-cut case, may actually be a symptom of an underlying bigger issue. The bigger issue could very well be or become a cultural issue for the organization if it is not attended too. Once the issue can be diagnosed, potential remedies can be suggested and implemented.

My assistant tried to get a hold of Rusty for two days. On Wednesday of that week, when I was told that we were still unable to reach him, I became worried enough to take further action. I got Rustys' address from the day captain, and took an afternoon drive out to his farm.

Rusty's farm was not as quaint as I had expected. He had a nice ranch style home and multiple large barns, that to this day I am curious what he had stored in them. I rung the front doorbell, waited, and then knocked. Just as I was about to walk away, Rusty's wife opened the door. I introduced myself and she invited me inside their home.

I was amazed by numerous war relics, photos, and models placed throughout their home. Rusty could have opened his own museum. I'd be willing to bet that he had a plane or two stored in those barns. Rusty's wife, Clair, informed me that she had only come home long enough to get some overnight items, and then she was heading back to the VA.

"Saturday evening, after coming home from the museum, Rusty was visibly agitated," Clair stated, "when he gets like that everything kind of comes unglued, and his health fails."

Devastated by this news I shared the incident at the museum with Clair. She shook her head knowingly, "I figured it was something like that."

She explained that Rusty has severe Post Traumatic Stress Disorder (PTSD) at times.[14] Ninety nine percent of the time he is a normally functioning individual, but it can only take one incident to throw him into a fit that can last for weeks. It seemed so obvious now, and I couldn't even believe that PTSD was something that we didn't at least investigate during our interview process.

Clair admitted that it was likely the P-51 that had set off this bout of PTSD. Apparently, every time he had contact with a Mustang since the war it had caused him issues. Clair also described all of her children and grandchildren, and how Rusty loved children and they adored him. It was becoming quite obvious that the visitors were not the issue, the plane was.

I made another faulty assumption sitting in the farmhouse that day. I assumed that there was no way that Rusty would want to ever return to the museum, nor would Clair let him. I apologized profusely for my oversight and tactlessness in my handling of the entire situation. Clair waved off my apologies. To my great surprise, she reassured me of Rustys' commitment and desire to serve the museum and inspire future aviators.

Absolutely floored, I humbly promised Clair that Rusty was welcome back to the museum at any time, and that we would do everything and anything that we could to support him. As Clair escorted me to my truck that day it occurred to me that I had been so obsessed with what Rusty was bringing to the museum that I had overlooked what the museum may be doing to or for Rusty.

Clair had told me in no uncertain terms that Rusty needed the museum. He needed the interaction, the comradery, he needed to feel useful, and I knew that as much as he needed us, we needed him. Now I had a new challenge; how could I use Rusty, but keep him safe?

Over the next month, I had a series of meetings with the volunteer day captains and senior museum staff. We had realized that we needed to completely rethink the way that we staffed our volunteers. We now understood that we were asking so much of them, assuming that they were simply happy to be there. No one was appropriately asking how we could make their volunteering a more pleasant and valuable experience. Thankfully it did not take an irreversible event to create this awareness, and I know once again that Rusty was proud to have been of service.

When Rusty returned to the museum we were much better prepared for him. Initially, we arranged a presentation for Rusty in the theater. He would show pictures, tell stories, and answer questions for our guests. This went on for weeks without a hitch. Eventually, Rusty requested to return to his station at the P-51 Mustang. There was hesitation. True to form, Rusty expected our concerns and was ready to put our fears at ease. He suggested that he be assigned a wingman to help him at the aircraft. The wingman had already agreed to be of service and keep our rowdy pilot under control; it worked.

Because Disabled Leaders understand that challenges exist, and are willing to explore why, they are able to turn liabilities into assets. Just as Rusty turned out to be an indispensable asset, disabled leaders can too. We just need to embrace the patience, understanding, and resolve to learn to develop and leverage our leader's capabilities.

Even when difficulties present themselves, matching pilots to airplanes is often far easier than developing leaders who are weak, or even worse, perceive themselves as weak. It is much easier to develop a weak leader than it is to change an internal perception that the leader is weak. The safe starting point is to remember that these perceptions were formed somewhere by something. It is unlikely that you will change a perception overnight or by merely telling the leader otherwise. Just as it takes time to build trust, in takes time to build understanding and acceptance.

When weaknesses aren't weaknesses

On the employee side of EAM, we also had interesting team dynamics. Around half of the staff were career professionals and the other half were high school students working, in many cases, their first job. Many of our younger employees worked part-time on the weekends, which I have mentioned before were our busiest days.

Evergreen had many programs to help these young leaders begin their careers, gain valuable experience, and even earn academic credits. EAM always strived to find ways to diversify its staff and leverage every employees' unique abilities. Enter Julie.

Julie was a very special young lady that I hired as a custodian. Julie was 17 years old and would come in each evening as the museum was closing and clean for two or three hours. It was a logical hire because Julie's mother worked for one of the operating companies, and did not get off of work until 7 p.m. Most evenings Julie would just sit in her mother's office and wait to go home. This was a win for everyone.

When Julie's mother approached me regarding her daughter interviewing for a custodian position, she was noticeably hesitant. At first, I thought perhaps she was worried about Julie having a job, impacting school, or evening possibly impacting her own job. Eventually, after a good five minutes of beating around the bush, mom said "I should warn you, Julie is on the Autism spectrum."

She went on to explain that Julie has incredible focus, work ethic, and dedication; however, she should not be interrupted once she has begun a task. Sometimes, if interrupted, Julie will have what her mother characterized as "a meltdown." Julie's mom described a few past situations to me to help me understand.

In the end, I was confident that Julie would do just fine. I assured her mother that Julie would be working with two other custodians who were friendly and understanding. We both agreed that we would give it a shot. I had one request; Julie would interview with me, for the experience.

Later that week I met with Julie and found her to be a pleasant and bright individual. I found it difficult to believe that Julie was autistic. As her mother had told me, Julie was a high performing autistic child. Julie accepted the position and was scheduled to start immediately.

Once Julie had been on the job for a week or so I ran into the lead custodian and asked how her new employee was doing. The lead was just as impressed as I was and raved about how quickly Julie had picked up on the schedule and processes. I was happy to report this to Julie's mother, who had been nervous.

As I would walk around at closing time, I would often wave to Julie from a distance, not wanting to approach her often and make her anxious. She was usually pushing a broom or a mop around with her, and almost always had a smile on her face. I would often see her reading the storyboards around the museum; which I thought was pretty neat.

One evening I spotted Julie leaning against a mop reading a storyboard as I had seen her before. A moment later the lead custodian came around the corner and I greeted her. I mentioned how nice it was to see Julie so interested in our mission. I immediately noticed a grimace on the leads face. I asked her what was wrong. She stammered for a few seconds, and then reluctantly told me her concerns. Julie had not been getting her work done. She spent much of her time on the clock reading about the displays. I then asked the lead if she had tried to correct Julie. She said almost every night she had asked Julie to complete tasks but was often ignored. I sensed hesitation. I immediately understood that the lead custodian was afraid of Julie's autism, and was worried that she would have a meltdown. I thanked the lead for her tactfulness and reassured her that she had done the right thing. I told her that I would go have a talk with Julie right then.

As I approached Julie, she quickly noticed me, and immediately lowered her head. "Hey Jules, pretty cool airplane huh?" I tried to ease her tension.

"Yessir, I like reading the stories," Julie responded with a little perk.

"Oh yeah," I asked, "how many have you read?"

"I think that I've read all of them," Julie stated with a proud smile.

"Wow, I wish more employees took so much interest in our displays, I'm proud of you," I encouraged, then added "just don't let it interfere to much with your work ok."

Julie assured me that she would not let her interest interrupt her duties, and I left things at that. I returned to the lead custodian and shared my confidence that Julie would be better focused on her job in the future. I also told her that I would check in to see how things were going the following week.

Imagine my surprise the following week when I received the report that Julie's behavior had not improved, but in fact had worsened. The lead custodian had actually done what she was afraid to do and attempted to reprimand Julie. Julie ran to her mother's office in tears. I decided that before we moved forward with any further punitive action, that I would go visit Julie's mother.

The moment I knocked on her door, Julie's mother gave me the *I know why you're here* look. I was surprised that practically before we had discussed anything, she said "I understand if you have to fire Julie."

I told Julie's mom that I don't think that the way to solve these types of problems is to terminate employment. I would rather find a solution that would benefit the organization and develop Julie at the same time. Julie's mom was unaccustomed to this approach, because in her environment, employees were fired and quit on a weekly basis. I assured her that we did not have the same culture at the museum.

First, we began by creating a shared understanding of the situation. Julie was not completing her assigned work because she was fascinated by the story boards. What her mom didn't know, was that I had encouraged Julie's obsession by applauding her initiative. What I didn't know was that Julie had taken her learning to a higher level after our interaction, and had begun checking out books from the library on the aircraft and wars they served. An additional concern for her mother was that Julie was staying up very late reading these books. In my mind the situation was evolving.

In Jim Collins' book, *Good to Great*, he acknowledges that sometimes we hire the right employees for the wrong job.[15] Using his analogy of a school bus, Collins shows us that sometimes the assigned seat doesn't work. Perhaps the individual is uncomfortable, or maybe he doesn't get along with his seatmate. Would you throw the individual off the bus, or try a different seat; perhaps multiple different seats? Disabled Leaders are quick to recognize when employees are struggling and will make the effort to figure out why. They remember a time when perhaps they themselves were struggling and may or may not have been offered assistance. disabled leaders will assume the worse, and make the situation far more painful than it needs to be. Most times our employees just need a little understanding or encouragement. Sometimes, a struggling employee will need a leader to help him realize his place in the organization. Disabled Leaders understand that every employee has something to offer their organization, and is willing to invest the time and effort to figure out what their role should be.

It would have been fairly easy just to go to Julie's mom and suggest that Julie wasn't ready for the responsibility of a job yet. She seemed somewhat apprehensive about the idea of Julie working in the first place. Consider what that action may have done to Julie though. Her confidence would have been shaken to say the least. It may have even compounded symptoms of her disability and sent her spiraling into a fit of depression. She may have never wanted to work or learn again.

Immediately resorting to extreme measures or discipline can have significant consequences for any employee, not only the disabled. It is unlikely that even the most engaging manager knows every aspect of each of their employees' lives. There could easily be external factors affecting your team's performance. I am not suggesting that you accept any excuse for every behavior or situation. I am merely asking you to take the time to consider what may be the cause of the issue, that you may be missing, and weigh multiple courses of action. A personal philosophy of mine is to be quick to offer compassion, but slow to initiate action. Disabled Leaders empathize with their employees and take time to fully understand the situation rather than act rashly.

Julie's initiative had inspired me more than any concern that the museum wasn't clean enough. I was determined to figure out a way to leverage the initiative, and also help Julie learn a lesson in responsibility. I formally scheduled a performance counseling session for Julie through her team lead. I knew that she would be scared, but if she showed up, I would be unable to question her resolve.

When it was time for our scheduled counseling, I was not the least bit surprised to see Julie knocking on my door. Yes, she looked like a deer in the headlights, but she was standing there. I was quite candid with Julie about the problem, and it was apparent that she understood. She did not make excuses, and she did not apologize. She seemed resigned to accept some form of punishment, and I think that she expected to be fired. I had a course of action in mind, but I was interested in what Julie thought first.

I asked Julie what she thought we should do about the situation. She just shrugged and said, "I don't know."

Next, I asked her "do you like working here?"

At this point I was merely hoping for a yes or no answer, so I was surprised when she provided a thoughtful response. "I like being at the museum more than sitting in my mom's office. I love learning about the airplanes. I love dusting the airplanes and keeping them pretty," with her response I felt like we were now getting somewhere.

I nodded my head understandingly. The next question would be the most difficult, "do you want to continue working for the museum?" I asked.

Julie sat quietly for a few seconds staring at the arm of her chair. Finally, she responded "I would like to keep working if you would let me," she said sheepishly.

I assured Julie that we absolutely valued her as a member of our team, and we hoped that she valued us too. I told her that a team can only succeed if every person is carrying their fair share. Julie acknowledged her shortcoming by sinking in the chair a littler lower. "I know that the museum is an exciting place and it can be easy to get distracted from your duties," I verbalized her thoughts then asked, "do you have any suggestions to help keep focused on your tasks?"

Julie thought for a moment. I could see her brain searching for a solution. It was encouraging to me that she was trying, and not just saying what she thought that I wanted to hear. The easy out would have sounded something like "yes boss, I promise to do a better job." How often do we get that level of authenticity from our employees? A better question might be, how can we ensure Julie's level of authenticity from our employees? I can't give you the perfect answer for each specific situation, but I can tell you what worked here, and has worked for me since.

Although Julie was young, and there are disability concerns, she still values honesty, like most people. From the first time that I met and hired Julie, I was always truthful and fair with her. I never treated her differently. When she walked into my office that day to face the music, she was scared. I didn't try to tell her that she was doing a good job, and then turn around and chastise her performance. By the time that we arrived at the point of conversation where we needed to derive a solution, I hope and believe that, she trusted me. She trusted that no matter what the outcome, I had her best interest at heart.

Disabled Leaders foster a trusting environment. Many times, they are forced to put their trust, and have almost a blind faith in other people. To disabled leaders this may sound absurd. I am an advocate of the trust but verify philosophy as well.[16] However, many times that verification may not come until it is too late to do anything about it. Imagine the wheelchair bound man trusting a random person to pull their chair up just three stairs. It's a blind trust, it must be. Why is this guy willing to help me up these stairs? Is he strong enough to do this? Does he know what he is doing? Can I trust him? In the three seconds between the question would you like help up these stairs, and the yes or no response, I doubt that the disabled person was able to consider each of those questions. **D**isabled **L**eaders have learned to trust first whereas disabled leaders would prefer to verify first.[17]

The "trust first" approach will empower your team. We all know that building trust takes time and commitment. However, it may take less time to build trust if we can learn to trust completely. It's a hard thing. Past experiences cloud our ability to trust openly and immediately. There is also a big difference between professional trust and personal trust. It is far easier to trust someone to complete their portion of a project than to trust them with your deepest darkest secrets. So, if professional trust is easier than personal trust, then why not start there. Of course, trust can and may be broken, but I believe that beginning with "trust first" will provide a solid foundation. If the employee feels like you trust them then they are likely to reciprocate that trust. It then becomes much more likely that you may someday share personal trust. Trust first professionally, empower your team, and the personal trust will form.

"Well Julie, I don't know the solution either, but I have some ideas. If you are willing to continue to try, then so am I, are you?"

"Yessir," Julie replied.

"Ok, it is important that you complete your responsibilities. I also want to encourage and reward your initiative. If you can get your jobs done each night, and you receive satisfactory reports from your team leader, I would like to offer you a weekend job with the education team," I stated trying to hold back my grin.

Julie perked up in her seat, "what do you mean?"

"If you can do the job that I initially hired you for, then I would like to offer you the opportunity to continue to learn and interact with the education team on the weekend," I restated.

Then added, "this way, hopefully knowing that you can read and learn on the weekends instead of during the cleaning hours, you will be able to focus on the cleaning that needs to be done."

Julie was ecstatic. She happily accepted my offer, and the solution worked beautifully. Julie would still sometimes stop and read a story board at night, but she was able to improve her efficiency to everyone's satisfaction. When I left EAM Julie was still working every weekend with the Boy Scouts and the Girl Scouts fulfilling her dreams and inspiring theirs.

As it turned out, Julie didn't have a disability at all. She just needed a little trust, some initiative, and maybe a little support. It is unlikely that a disabled leader would have discovered Julie's talent or ambition. Too often they only see the surface. disabled leaders might see the problem but fail to see a win/win solution. Disabled Leaders build trust first that enables them to collaborate, and ultimately create a team environment.

A collaborative team environment built on trust ultimately begins with self-awareness. Understanding where you are and how to develop your strengths and weaknesses will promote openness and honesty within yourself and your team. Next, it may help to know where you are going.

Building Disabled Platforms

Disabled Leaders spend more time thinking about what they CAN do as opposed to focusing on what they cannot do. disabled leaders' dwell on what they consider the impossible, and become accustomed to making excuses for their failure. Disabled Leaders envision the possibilities, even when they appear to be improbable, and figures out how to make them a reality.

Kortney Clemons dreamed to be a professional football player. It wasn't a farfetched dream. Kortney was a high school all-star. He was powerful, and he was fast. More importantly, he was dedicated. The only setback was Kortney's size. College recruiters were impressed with his athleticism, strength, and vision; but to play at the next level, at 5'10", he was simply undersized.

Kortney was able to overcome concerns of his size and play football in college, but this story isn't about that. Kortney had just begun football season when 9/11 happened. Like many other heroes, Kortney felt called to serve. He left his football career, his dream, behind to serve a higher purpose.

Kortney not only served his country, but he also sacrificed for it. In 2005 Kortney lost a leg to an Improvised Explosion Device (IED). You can read Kourtney's amazing story in his book *Amped: A Soldier's Race for Gold in the Shadow of War*. What I want you to think about is the power of sacrificing for something larger than yourself. Larger might mean your family, your community, or maybe even your country. To risk everything and end up severely disabled, what would you do?

It's hard to say until it happens to you. Even some of the most resilient leaders I know could buckle and break under the stress of sustaining a disability. Waking up one day to a soundless world, a dark world, unable to move, unable to speak, or unable to think. It all seems surreal and improbable, but it happens every day.

Of course, many disabled people cannot cope with their tragedy such. They lose focus on the light in their life. Everything that they have left to live for and accomplish slips away from them as they helplessly lose control of their reality. But, how can you maintain control of your life when horrible things happen to you? Why do some people appear to thrive after enduring a life-changing event while others fall apart? To examine those questions, let's further consider my friend Kortney Clemons.

Let's be honest, most people do not even have a dream. Sure, there are things that we hope to do some day, but that isn't necessarily a legitimate dream. A dream is something more. It is passion. It is prose. To make a dream tangible takes incredible planning, insight, dedication, and persistence. One does not simply wake up with a dream one day, and the next have it come to fruition.

Imagine you have a dream. You worked for it every day for years. Countless hours preparing for the day that your dream will become a reality. Now imagine that in one second or with one decision that dream is destroyed. You have a decision: let the dream that dies destroy you or use the death of that dream to aspire a new one.

Kortney knew once he lost his leg that he would not be able to play college football anymore. That dream was dead. Kortney was not. He knew that many people thought that he was too small to play football. He was able to prove them wrong with his athleticism and speed. Kortney still believed that his athleticism was a strength.

Speed was a different challenge. First, he had to learn to walk again, let alone run.

Instead of letting his dream completely die, against all odds, Kortney was determined to slightly shift his aspirations. He was now going to compete in the Paralympics. While football, and eventually track, was Kortney's passion, it was also a means to an end. Indeed, Kortney had earned the GI Bill, and other resources to help pay for his study and development. He would see his education through as well, last earning a master's degree at The University of Kansas while running on the track team.

First place ribbons, gold medals, and graduate degrees. All of Kortney's dreams came true, although he had to adapt them a little. He excelled in a sport, at the international level, and received an advanced education. All of this, although he never played another down of football.

Instead of throwing down his cards, Kortney played the hand he was dealt. He leveraged what he learned in the military by accepting risk and exercising initiative. In this case, accepting risk also meant accepting harsh realities. His leg was gone. Kortney was able to take that weakness, and turn it into a strength, which allowed him to build his platform. Disabled Leaders accept risk and exercise initiative to build platforms that will allow them to excel despite their handicap.

Disabled Leaders accept risk in almost every action or decision that they make. Of course, there are different levels of risk. Certainly, there is the risk of injury if the person attempts something foolish or a feat beyond their ability. There is also often a great risk of embarrassment, which I have found can be just as damaging as a physical injury. What enables Disabled Leaders to accept risk in situations where disabled leaders may not?

Disabled Leaders know no failure, and disabled leaders know failure. The difference is that Disabled Leaders are able to mitigate, leverage, and overcome failure. Too often disabled leaders fail because they were not prepared to fail. Disabled Leaders understand that sometimes failure is inevitable, often they've experienced it. I know that sometimes my Cochlear Implant is going to go haywire, Kortney knows that sometimes his prosthetic leg is going to seize up, Stephanie knows that sometimes she is going to trip over something, but we can't and won't let that risk slow us down. We either plan for or accept the inevitable. We learn lessons, sometimes the hard way, but we learn.

As **D**isabled **L**eaders learn, they build; get better and stronger. disabled leaders discount their failures and pretend they didn't happen.[18] Consequently, they cannot learn from their mistakes, which greatly increases the risk of it happening again. Albert Einstein, a **D**isabled **L**eader, is credited with saying "insanity is doing that same thing over and over again and expecting different results." That sounds like a handicap to me. How do **D**isabled **L**eaders avoid such a serious handicap?

It starts with attitude. I once had a mentor who liked to inspire his employees and community members by stating "Anything you can conceive, you must believe, then you can achieve." I call this the CBA Platform. Take a moment to re-read and understand the simple brilliance of this concept. Conceive. Believe. Achieve. Three simple words, a simple concept, not such an easy process.

I bet as soon as you read CBA you thought of a brilliant idea you once had or conceived. You may have believed in the idea with all your heart, maybe you still do. Did that idea ever become action? Was it successful? Why? Why not? When **D**isabled **L**eaders have good ideas, they will do whatever it takes to make them a reality, because they believe in the idea, they believe in themselves, and they believe in others. disabled leaders are capable of having ideas, but often will find themselves incapable of maintaining the will to see the concept to fruition because they may not believe in themselves or others.

Consider everything that Kortney had to do to build his CBA Platform. Conceive: First he had to accept the reality of his situation. He lost his leg, he would receive a prosthetic, hundreds of hours of physical therapy, family care, new career, the list could go on and on; but despite the seemingly endless setbacks, Kortney was still capable of finding a goal.

Believe: The first time he told his family that he was going to be a track star, I bet he got some sideways looks and possibly outright negativity. I imagine the white gloves approach, "Kortney, let's just focus on getting better, and learning to walk first. What are you going to do for a job to support your family? How do you plan to run competitively; its impossible!" Believing is the toughest step of CBA by far. Even if you believe in yourself

100% there will always be someone who does not; whether they say it or not.[19]

When I enrolled in my first term of college, after retiring from the Army, and submitted my course load to the Vocational Rehab Counselor, he said "NO". He looked at me incredulously for selecting four classes in one term. He told me that I should only take one class per term, at least for the first year or two. I responded, "sir, it would take me fifteen years to graduate at that rate!" The bottom line of that conversation is that I believed in myself, but he did not. He probably had good reasons for his philosophy. He had probably seen many veterans do the same thing, only to fail. But I was not going to fail, because I believed in myself; I was a **D**isabled **L**eader.

Kortney is a **D**isabled **L**eader too. He had conceived an idea, made it a goal, and now he believed in it. No one could stop him from achieving his goal. Only one person even had that capability at this point; himself. Once a **D**isabled **L**eader believes in an idea or a goal, no one can stop her from achieving that goal except for herself.

Achieve: Kourtney believed in the goal and he believed in himself. Those are the two main ingredients for achievement. But, not the only ingredients! If I were making a cake, I would need more than flour and sugar. Disabled Leaders have determination. Imagine strapping on metal legs for the first time, and then attempting to stand. Imagine walking. Imagine running.

It is difficult for me, and probably most other people, to imagine walking on anything other than our own two legs. Part of my own traumatic brain injury (TBI) was the destruction of my vestibular system. The vestibular system controls balance. I had to learn how to stand, walk, run(ish), swim and many other basic functions from scratch. I am a big guy. Bigger now than I was then, and not for the better. I remember the discomfort of having a one-hundred-pound rehabilitation therapist responsible for steadying my two-hundred-and-thirty-pound frame during exercises. Most days I wanted to quit. Simple exercises such as standing on a pillow and slowly turning my head from one side to the other was a very humbling task, even for an Airborne Ranger. There was only one way to improve and overcome—determination.

In addition to believing and having determination, Disabled Leaders must also persevere. Even with a great level of determination, there will be setbacks. What happens when we fall down determines the difference between disabled leaders and Disabled Leaders. disabled leaders find reasons to stay down, not get up, or lose determination. Disabled Leaders hope for the best but plan for the worst. Disabled Leaders understand that determination is unlikely to succeed without perseverance.

How many times did Kortney fall down; figuratively and literally? How often was he uncomfortable? How many times was he told "no, you can't do that?" More importantly, how many times did he keep pushing on. I don't know the number, but I do know that he kept pushing. He pushed all the way to the finish line; in Beijing, for a Gold Medal!

Achievement, will be situational. I have identified two major traits that Disabled Leaders demonstrate to achieve their goals: dedication and perseverance. Obviously, there are more ingredients that we can add to make different or better cakes. Examples include: resilience and motivation, and we will examine these closer in later chapters. What other traits do you exhibit as a Disabled Leader?

It isn't difficult to understand how Kourtney built his CBA Platform. Hopefully you find the CBA useful yourself. There is something else interesting about Kortney's CBA Platform which you may not have considered. While Kortney was assessing his strengths and weaknesses, which column do you think he listed running in? Better yet, which column would you list running in, if you had just lost your leg? Truthfully, I don't know if he considered his running ability a weakness or a strength at first, but I am sure that he could envision the possibilities, down the road.

It would be logical to want to build your CBA Platform on a strength. For many leaders that approach makes perfect sense; leverage your strengths for max production and potential. Nevertheless, I beg you to consider the power of building your CBA Platform on a weakness. Wow! Taking the thing that you are worst at, or the perception which is holding you back, and use it as a launching platform. It may be difficult to fathom at first, but building a weakness into a tool for success is incredibly empowering, especially for Disabled Leaders.

If I haven't mentioned it lately, I'm deaf. I sacrificed my hearing in Afghanistan in 2004 to small arms fire. I have a Cochlear Implant (CI) on one ear that allows me to perceive many sounds in a reasonable and quiet environment. I have attended several hearing loss conventions over the years and have noticed certain stigmas changing. For example, when I first got the CI, many in the Deaf community were not happy with the technology. The believed that the technology was infringing on their culture. Over the years, I notice that more people in the Deaf community have become accepting to this miraculous technology. This technology is wonderful, especially for people like me who were not raised in the Deaf culture, but endured a significant life changing event, that perhaps we were not ready for. So, for the confused readers, Kourtney doesn't have both legs, but he can walk; and I don't have hearing, but I can hear; selectively.

In both of these cases, Kourtney and I built our CBA Platforms from what many would consider our weaknesses. Instead of letting the disability or weakness define us, we decided to define it. *Lt. Dan you don't got any legs....cool, I'm gonna be a gold medalist Olympian then...*

Our friend Tom can't hear anymore, what should he do now? I doubt that many people thought that I would go on to run major organizations, receive graduate degrees, and listen to people for a living. How does one even accomplish that? Easily, because I didn't let a disability define me. Instead I chose to leverage it.

One of the first things I learned as a newly deaf person was how to listen. From teaching, mentoring, and coaching thousands of executives over the past ten years, I am convinced many people could learn how to listen better if they lost their hearing.

I was not able to receive my Cochlear Implant (CI) immediately after I became deaf. It took about one year for the swelling in my brain to subside enough to try the procedure. I wouldn't trade that year for anything. I learned more about myself in that one year than I did in ten years of college. It was during this time that I learned what effective communication looks and sounds like.

In the leadership courses that I teach, I describe effective communication as simple as possible. There are two parts: what we say and what we hear. Remember it as two sides of a coin. It is a far simpler description than what Army doctrine provides, but I think that it resonates easier, and maybe even better.

Fortunately, although I could not hear at all during this year, I could speak. Speaking accurately, clearly, and precisely became essential to being able to get anyone to attempt to have a conversation with me. Can you guess why? Because to respond to me, the other person had to write down what they wanted to say. I didn't know sign language yet, and none of my friends, family, or caretakers did either. This was before everyone had smart phones. I had to carry a notebook, or my favorite, a white board on a string around my neck, in order for people to be able to communicate with me. I learned that people get tired of writing very quickly. One General (disabled leader), who will remain nameless, handed me back my white board and suggested that I write to him. Concisely presenting my thoughts, ideas, and emotions became an important aspect of maintaining contact with the rest of the world.

Disabled Leaders provide clear expectations in order to create shared understanding. Disabled Leaders learn early on that presenting their needs in a clear and efficient fashion is often important to their survival. I offer that the same can be said for organizations. Consider a person with severe allergies that needs a person, with no knowledge of their disability, to retrieve and administer their EpiPen. They have put great thought into this situation and have a plan to clearly communicate their exact needs. There is no time for confusion or miscommunication. It is literally a life or death situation. Would your organization survive?

More importantly than what we say is what we hear. When I ask my students what effective communication or creating shared understanding consists of, I almost always hear active listening.[20] That answer is exactly right, doctrinally. Active listening has become a well-known buzz term in executive service and is almost always used in leadership discussions, but what does it mean? Most executives agree that active listening consists of being engaged in a conversation. That answer isn't wrong. However, some executives (disabled leaders) think being engaged in the conversation means dominating the discussion. That doesn't sound like active listening to me.

So, how does one listen actively? Body language is a common answer. Certainly, appearing interested helps. Eye contact suggests that the receiver is paying attention. Posture could send messages as to how much the receiver cares. Asking questions of clarity, in order to gain understanding, indicates interest. Paraphrasing ensures shared understanding of the intent. Note, I said paraphrasing, not parroting. disabled leaders parrot in order to appease the presenter, but **D**isabled **L**eaders paraphrase to ensure they understand the purpose or intent of the idea or action.

Active listening is something that most executives appear to believe in, but few accomplish easily. That is why I often suggest to them that the best way to become an active listener is to become deaf. If I just triggered you, I apologize. No one ever told me I was a good listener until I became deaf. I can't hear. To be honest, I'm glad, I don't want to hear, hearing sucks. The best part of my day is turning off my CI. Most of what we hear is noise. It is nothing. It is distraction at best. Imagine being able to tune all of that out and being able to truly listen. Yes, it is a pain sometimes. I don't even try in noisy environments, but that is the point. Neither should you. In order to listen, and create shared understanding, **D**isabled **L**eaders foster and ensure suitable environments. Environments that are more conducive to creating shared understanding.

Environments where people can be heard, respected, and appreciated.

While the success stories I have shared here belong to Kortney and myself, there are many others. I'm not sure if this is a profoundly new perspective or approach, obviously we accomplished these things without any formal knowledge of this process, but developing a weakness into a launching pad for success works. It may seem to some that we used this approach for glory and self-satisfaction, but I will tell you that this is not true. Yes, it has been an amazing journey for us, one that we hope is just beginning, but even more so, we hope that our success stories inspire other **D**isabled **L**eaders to continue their own stories.

Building our CBA Platforms from weaknesses worked tremendously for Kortney, and myself. Developing your weakness into your greatest strength could be incredibly empowering for you too. It will be one of your biggest challenges for sure, but the reward for achievement will be far greater than you could imagine. I encourage you to go back to chapter two and review your weaknesses. Which is your biggest weakness? How can you overcome it? Even better, how can you leverage it?

Build Your CBA Platform

Greatest weakness:

_____

_____

Why does this disable me?

_____

_____

Reasons to:

Mitigate: **Build:**

1._____   1._____

2._____   2._____

3._____   3._____

Conceive (Goal): _____

_____

Believe (How): _____

_____

Achieve (Outcomes): _____

_____

Empowering Disabled Leaders

Disabled Leaders are not born with superpowers. Well, ok, maybe some are, I hope. What I mean is, Disabled Leaders learn to rise to the occasion and leverage their full potential, but they almost never do it alone. I cannot think of a single person who has achieved greatness entirely on their own. We need help. We need each other. Disabled Leaders understand empowerment better than anyone else. We appreciate other's willingness to assist, in any way, in achieving our goals. In this chapter we will investigate empowerment. What is empowerment? Why is empowerment important to Disabled Leaders? How can Disabled Leaders empower others the way that they have been empowered?

Let's start with the most difficult question first, what is empowerment? If you look up the term empowerment in a dictionary you will likely find a definition which states *giving power to someone to do something.* If that answer seems simple enough to you, well, you are right, it is simplistic. Empowerment can be much more, and it can be much less. That is both the beauty and the madness of empowerment. An action or an idea that may empower one leader may not empower another leader, it is highly subjective.[21]

For example, a **D**isabled **L**eader, in an attempt to build trust and empower his team, tells them that they can exercise a flexible work schedule. Because he knows the people on his team live very different lives, he wants them to feel comfortable juggling their responsibilities. He tells the team that they can work whatever hours they would like, as long as they put in their eight hours a day. Several members of the team feel empowered by this new policy. Now they do not have to worry about how their kids will get to soccer practice or being home in time to sign for that important package. They are empowered to take responsibility for their own time management and priorities. This may result in greater productivity and improve general happiness in the office.

A couple of the team members are not empowered by the new policy. One member already came and went as she needed, and therefore doesn't see any difference. Another member is opposed to the new policy because he feels like it is too lax, and people will take advantage by not putting in their eight hours a day, thereby creating stress on other team members.

Here we have one action, with good intention, meant to empower a team. Some of the team was empowered, and some of the team weren't. Both sides had good reasons for their reactions. How might the Disabled Leader encourage his empowering action to have the results that were intended? That is, how can he empower the other two?

Truthfully, it is very difficult to ensure empowerment. However, we can do more than simply offer it. While your actions may be obvious to you, it is important to discuss the purpose with the team. Instead of just informing the team that they have flexible work hours, tell the reason WHY you think it is important. Attempt to have a candid discussion about the value of your empowerment initiative. If there are naysayers, hear their concerns. Wait, don't hear, LISTEN to their concerns. Ask questions. Make sure you really understand. You may need to rethink the initiative after this discussion. You might even weigh the pros and cons in a transparent setting. Even if you have to change the plan, your team will appreciate you including them in the discussion and making them feel a part of the decision. You will have empowered them ad hoc.

Military Empowerment called Mission Command

Over the past decade I have had the honor of helping the US Army develop their understanding of empowerment, and how it should play a role in the agency. The Army's term for empowerment is Mission Command. It is the Army's leadership philosophy, or our approach to leading, if you will. It is also more than our approach to leading; it is why we lead. The Army defines Mission Command a little differently than the definition of empowerment that you might find in the dictionary. Army Doctrine Publication (ADP) 6-0 defines Mission Command as the exercise of authority and direction, by the commander [leader], using mission orders [guidance] to enable disciplined initiative within the commander's intent [purpose] to empower agile and adaptive leaders... That is a very wordy way of saying empowerment. I often tell my students that the reason they are stuck with me for the next four weeks is because the Army wants to empower them to be the best leaders that they can be (**D**isabled **L**eaders, but the term hasn't caught on yet).

Other than the military lingo used to describe empowerment, another question arises. Does the military, or private organizations, really want to empower its employees with authority and decisionmaking? How much should we, as **D**isabled **L**eaders, empower our employees or colleagues? The Army had the foresight to apply constraints to its empowerment model. Constraints may seem disempowering, but they can actually serve to strengthen empowerment. The Army applied six principles to Mission Command to help describe and understand the process. They are fairly intuitive but let's make sure that we share a reasonable common understanding of each. I also encourage you to check out ADP 6-0; it's worth a google.

1. Build Cohesive Teams Thru Mutual Trust (professional and personal)
2. Create Shared Understanding (boy that sounds familiar)
3. Provide Clear Commanders Intent (Purpose or Why)

4. Exercise Disciplined Initiative (Disciplined refers to staying within guidance)

5. Use Mission Orders (Guidance or right and left limits)

6. Accept Prudent Risk (Make sure the juice is worth the squeeze)

Some readers are thinking, "great, but I am not in the military." Well, maybe you should be! Just kidding, but I hope that we all understand that these principles are just as easily applicable outside of the Army too. These six principles give us a good starting point for understanding how we can empower our teams. As I describe each principle, think about how you already apply it or can apply it, or even better, develop it.

The first principle is to **build cohesive teams thru mutual trust**. While the outcome of establishing mutual trust is to build cohesive teams (for the Army), trust is a focal point in empowerment. **D**isabled **L**eaders must build trust within their team in order to be able to empower them. disabled leaders will attempt to "empower" their team to build trust. Trust must come first. Empowerment will not appear authentic or last long if trust does not already exist. Absolutely, building trust is on ongoing process, but there must be a healthy level of trust present before empowerment can occur.

In chapter two we discussed **D**isabled **L**eaders' trusting nature, and how it empowers them. Now we are building that concept, evolving that **D**isabled **L**eaders also empower others to trust. Remember, **D**isabled **L**eaders trust first and value personal trust; whereas disabled leaders are content with stopping at professional trust.

Building trust, as an action, within a team is the easiest thing that a **D**isabled **L**eader can do to empower them. Building trust, as a process, is the most difficult necessity to empower. That is because people are different. There are often extreme dynamics within a team. **D**isabled **L**eaders value the diversity within their teams, but must also figure out how to manage it in order to empower. That is why we came up with mission statements, visions, and organizational values. These approaches give us a common starting point. Where we diverge is in our personal values.

Recall our initiative for open work hours? When I first had the idea, it appeared genius to me. Something that everyone would be happy with. However, there were a couple of issues with the empowerment initiative. First, I thought the initiative was certain to make everyone happy. Steve Jobs put it nicely *if you want to make everyone happy, don't be a leader, sell ice cream.* It didn't occur to me that personal values might conflict. Some of the team valued the proposed flexibility. Some of the team valued structured hours. Lastly, some of the team valued autonomy (remember the person who already did what she wanted). It would not be fair to assume that any of these three groups do not value responsibility. The other issue was trust.

As the team leader, it could be assumed that, I tried to build trust by empowering. Perhaps I overestimated how much the team trusts each other. Maybe I trust my team more than they trust each other. Either way, the mistake became quickly apparent. The **D**isabled **L**eader quickly opened dialog and addressed concerns.

Creating a shared understanding of purpose can build trust. Although it may not always build trust, at least it is less likely to break trust. So, the **D**isabled **L**eader told the team that he wanted to ensure that everyone is comfortable with their responsibilities. He believes that trusting the team with their own responsibilities (time management) will improve effectiveness and efficiency within the organization. Through open dialog and discourse, the **D**isabled **L**eader further inspires the flexible group and calms the rigid group. Allowing both parties to voice their concerns brought ease to the team. The **D**isabled **L**eader provided a formal platform to openly discuss the initiative so that all sides could share their opinions. The team decided to try the initiative for one quarter and then reassess, and more importantly, they built trust in the process.

As I mentioned earlier, team dynamics are diverse because we all hold different personal values. Organizations try to find commonality by implementing organizational values. So, that begs the question, what kind and how much trust do we need to be a high performing team? Most teams do have a high level of professional trust. They trust each other to show up and get their work done to the best of their ability. Is that enough? What about personal trust though? Should teammates trust each other enough to be comfortable with engagements outside of work? Can we grab a beer after work? Do you want to go to the game this weekend? Could you watch my child for a few hours while I run an errand? Will you help me bury the body? Professional trust accomplishes the mission, but personal trust improves the organization. How much trust is enough for your team?

High performing teams require some balance of professional and person trust. The professional trust is easy, either you have it, or you don't. Building personal trust requires some level of awareness of your teams' abilities and ambitions. How much trust is enough to encourage the team to believe and invest in each other? I have created four levels of personal trust:

1. **Invite**- Do you wanna grab a beer after work?
2. **Accept**- Hey guys, I have tickets to the game this weekend for anyone who wants to go with me.
3. **Leverage**- I'm in a bind, would you be able to babysit for a few hours?
4. **Commit**- Who will help me bury the body?

Let's be realistic, you can't just jump to level four. No one is going to help you bury a body without a beer first. If you invite trust, and it is accepted, then you can leverage it to get the team to commit. A committed team is a high performing team. High performing teams improve the organization, and sometimes, they change the world.

In chapter one I proposed that everyone has been disabled at some point in their life, by fear. The same goes for teams. Teams fear the unknown of the change. Building trust is essential to conquering fear. Some managers (<u>d</u>isabled <u>l</u>eaders) believe that fear is a leadership style; it's not. In the military, some managers try to use fear as a motivator. While fear may get immediate results, in the larger arena it can paralyze the entire organization. Ultimately, everyone will become too afraid to sustain success.

Building trust eliminates fear. Building trust will alleviate doubts and concerns of what will happen if by chance there is some level of failure. If the team trusts that each member will shoulder his share of the task, then there is no need for fear or concern. If the team trusts that the manager has their best interest at heart and will fairly supervise the initiative, then there is nothing to fear. 21

Disabled Leaders understand that building trust is not a one and done deal. disabled leaders will be content with holding an annual team building and then even declaring trust is built. I teach an elective course at the Army Management Staff College that I have titled *Building Trust with a Baseball Bat.* As the title infers, disabled leaders believe that they can force trust, but Disabled Leaders train the process and trust the process.

I begin the class the way every heroic teacher in the history of cinema does, I write my name on the whiteboard. Then I ask a question which they probably aren't expecting: by show of hands, do you trust me? A few seconds of confusion and doubt pass then a few hands pop up. Ok, you trust me, why? A typical answer is, they wouldn't let just anyone teach this class. (Boy are they in for a disappointment.) Ok, what about the folks who didn't raise their hand, why don't you trust me? Typical answer, I don't know you. Fair enough.

Next, I tell the class that we are going to play a game for the duration of the course. When I ask *How's Trust* the students will indicate that it has increased with a thumbs up, decreased with a thumbs down, or no change by staring at me blankly like I'm an idiot.

Then, I add the prefix to my name, "Dr." How's trust? Inevitably, at least one person who hadn't trusted me before will give a thumbs up. What changed? Typical answers, credibility and competence. So, then what about you guys who still refuse to give me a chance? Typical answer, we are more interested in your character. Half the class trusts me because of my perceived credibility and competence, and the other half does not trust me because of my lack of character. Rough room!

It is always a fun discussion with a little hard ribbing, but we always take away the same thing. Credibility and competence can only get me so far before I will need to show some character.[23] I need to know that you will do what you say. On the other hand, I can only wear so many stylish suits, buy so many lunches, or tell so many jokes before I will need to prove that I know what I am doing. Man, trust is fickle! There has to be a balance. **D**isabled **L**eaders figure out how to create that balance. As the class is winding down, I ask one last time *How's Trust?* Usually, I get an overwhelming number of thumbs up. As **D**isabled **L**eaders, I hope that you ask this question every day going forward, even if you only ask yourself; How's Trust?

The second principle is **create shared understanding**. At the end of the last chapter we touched on the importance of creating shared understanding. You may recall that I listed two important functions of creating shared understanding: providing clear expectations (what we say) and active listening (what we hear). Immediately we start to see clear connections between these principles. In the last section, on building trust, I demonstrated the importance of creating shared understanding. If providing clear expectations sounds familiar as well, it is because I use it synonymously with the next principle, Provide Clear Commanders (leaders) Intent, which I will discuss in that section. All of this is connected.

It is one thing to say provide clear expectations, but it is another feat to accomplish it. I know a married couple, both are **D**isabled **L**eaders, who struggled with what it means to provide clear expectations. Picture the following…..

The setting is Kansas City during winter. A storm has just moved through the city which has left thirteen inches of snow in the family's driveway. It is seven degrees outside, but the husband knows that the driveway must be cleared in case of an emergency situation. He is from the south and every minute of the hour, that it takes to shovel the driveway, slowly freezes his soul. Finally, he's finished. He walks back thru the garage and prepares to enter the house thru the garage door. As he opens the door, a blast of warm air hits him, followed by a shrill voice from upstairs: *I just mopped the floor!!!* Just as quickly as the warm air overtook him so does a feeling of defeat, frustration, and disappointment. He had just spent the last hour outdoors, breaking his back, where hell had obviously frozen over, and all he wanted was to be warm, a drink of water, and perhaps a little appreciation. If she was insinuating a competition, shoveling the driveway surely beat mopping the floor.

So, he shook off her words and made his way across the kitchen for a glass of water. Unbeknownst to him, behind him trailed ice, snow, and mud. As he was drinking his glass of water he turned around, and there she stood, she was angry, but why?

The women reading this are mad now too. So, I ask again, why is she mad? He tracked up the floor she just mopped! She told him she just mopped it. It seems obvious right? What did she not tell him? Did she set a clear expectation not to mess up her floor? (Ladies, don't break anything yet, I swear, vengeance will be yours, just wait.) We can make an assumption that she meant to not walk on the floor that she had just cleaned, but it may not be as obvious as you think. What was he supposed to do, sit in the freezing garage until the floor was dry or he was dry? What initially appears to be a clear expectation turns out to be an assumption, at best, with many potential courses of action.

If she wanted to create a clear expectation, no matter the environment or the location, then she should have been clear in her directions and desires. How is this for a clear expectation? *Honey, I just mopped, please take off your snow gear in the garage so that you don't mess up the floor.* What is the difference between that statement and the original?

Have you ever heard of the five W's: who, what, when, where, and why?[24] The original statement only had the *what*. I just mopped the floor. The what, without any support, is worthless. Don't roll your eyes at me, I just proved that point. Let's see what happens as we add some more W's. Honey *(who)*, I just mopped *(what)*, please take off your snow gear *(what)*, in the garage *(where)*, so that you don't mess up the floor *(why)*. Now, which of those statements are more clear? Which is more effective? Fine, if the "honey" is driving you crazy, then get rid of it. Did it change anything? Perhaps the tone, which is important, but it is still more clear.

When **D**isabled **L**eaders aren't asking for clarity, we are creating it. The five W's is a simple model that goes a long way toward creating clear expectations. As you start to implement this model, at work or at home, strive to include as many of the W's as possible. You won't always need to cover every W. In different situations different W's will carry more value in the information. In this statement, which W was the most important? Some may argue the where, but I would wager it is the why. The why, or the purpose is often a key element in creating clarity. We will discuss the why more in the next principle.

And now, vengeance for the ladies. Fast forward six months. Same couple same home. The big difference is that now there is a heat wave and it is in the triple digits outside. Once again, the husband has done his duty, and push mowed the entire yard. He is nearly having a heat stroke. He comes into the cool air-conditioned house, flips on the ceiling fan, and plops down into his cool leather recliner. A minute later his wife comes downstairs, looking as beautiful and refreshed as ever. (No, the dirty floor didn't kill her and no she didn't kill him.) The husband looks up at his loving wife from the recliner and says *I am about to have a heat stroke, boy an iced tea sure would be nice.* The wife smiles back at him knowingly and says *you're right honey, that does sound nice, please get me one too.*

See, the wife learned her lesson about creating clear expectations, and now, I bet the husband will too. All jokes aside, how many times have you received an email with a task, that was just the bare minimum; *get this done.* At first glance, you might think, boy that is empowering, that is what trust looks like. After a few times of receiving tasks like that, you may find that you might not maintain that point of view. Get this done. Ok, what is my timeline, is anyone helping me, and most importantly if we want to empower you, why or what is the purpose? Disabled Leaders understand when and how to leverage empowerment. Yes, sometimes it will be more beneficial to just say get this done, and you might add, however you want, if you need anything don't hesitate to ask. Other times, it would be greatly appreciated if you provide as much detail, and as many resources as possible. Both can be empowering, but there has to be a conscious balance.

Number three, **provide clear commanders** (leader) **intent**, the purpose or the why, is a constraint to empowerment. It keeps the user from doing something for nothing, or just as bad, doing the completely wrong thing. Often disabled leaders will focus on a task without understanding the purpose behind it. When he doesn't understand the purpose of the task there is a much greater chance for failure. Disabled Leaders take the time and employ their active listening skills to ensure that they understand the purpose of everything they do. Creating shared understanding of the purpose ensures Disabled Leaders are successful in their efforts. Disabled Leaders provide purpose.[25]

Although clear intent is a constraint, by design, it is still significantly empowering. It is not just the Disabled Leader ensuring that their team is doing the right thing. It can, and should also be, the team helping the Disabled Leader with understanding the purpose. Many times, during the course of a project, the purpose evolves. disabled leaders often only understand and accept the initial intent, and sometimes do not see or think about the problem again until the team returns with a solution. The issue with this approach is that the problem may have changed. The team may have uncovered new information in the form of facts, assumptions, or opinions. The problem has developed. Consequently, the purpose may have developed too. Disabled Leaders provide purpose and understand the process impacts the purpose and it may change. So, they check in regularly in order to maintain shared understanding. This helps Disabled Leaders solve the actual problem, instead of only curing symptoms.

Many Disabled Leaders find their empowerment in purpose. A sense of purpose can give us a will to overcome and strive to succeed in almost anything. The purpose may be quite personal. My purpose may be to walk again or talk again. Something that most people take for granted every day. Perhaps that purpose is something we feel that we need for survival. That purpose can provide sheer will to accomplish the impossible. Even hoping to build a better life for my kids. A purpose could also be a wish or desire. It may not be a life or death scenario, but it is something important about who we want to be. Maybe I want to get an education, write a book, or start a company. I will leverage these goals to achieve my purpose. Having a purpose, knowing the purpose, and understanding our purpose is a powerful approach.

Principle four is **exercise disciplined initiative**. Based on what you just read, **D**isabled **L**eaders empower their teams through purpose, and vice versa. By allowing or encouraging the team to work the problem and develop the purpose, the **D**isabled **L**eader is influencing initiative.[26]

Disabled **L**eaders don't only encourage initiative, but also exercise it themselves. There are different ways to consider initiative, contextually. Most commonly, initiative can mean starting something on your own, without a formal prompt. Often, this initiative is derived from empowerment. Initiative must be rewarded and not punished in order to be empowering. It is unlikely you will get more initiative if previous initiative was chided. disabled leaders can unknowingly disempower initiative by blowing up a failure. If an initiative fails, a **D**isabled **L**eader will make sure that it is used as a learning experience, accept responsibility, and attempt to salvage as much as possible.

For some **Di**sabled **Le**aders, initiative also means imagination. Imagination means creating something new. More often than I like to admit, I find that my students confuse creative thinking with critical thinking. When I introduce critical thinking, typically a student will remark about thinking outside of the box. Critical thinking is really about expanding the box; making it bigger. Critical thinking is doing everything that you can to better understand a concept or idea. Creative thinking is thinking outside of the box or developing a concept or idea.

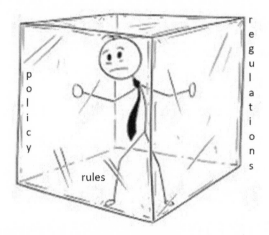

The Army will not like this, but we are stuck in the box. We have built a huge box and continue expanding it, but at the end of the day, we are still inside of the box. It's just so comfortable in there. We have padded the walls, floors, and ceiling with policy, regulation, and rules. I often tell my classes that I have seen the problem, and he is me. So, how do I get out of the box? Through creative thinking! There are two prominent types of creative thinking: deductive and inductive. Deductive thinking is using prior experience or knowledge to create something new. Inductive thinking is creating something new from nothing.[27] An inductive idea may not actually be a new concept, but it is new to the thinker, they actually conceived it themselves. Disabled Leaders value each of these approaches to achieve a greater whole called mental agility.

How can empowerment leverage imagination to inspire initiative? When I draw the stick figure in the box, I always joke that he stays in the box because he is naked. To get him the leave the box, we have to get him some clothes, so let's start with an easy accessory; a hat.

Edward De Bono has created a powerful tool that can be used to align team processes, called the Six Hats Thinking Process.[28] The Six Thinking Hats process has been used all over the world by mega corporations to academic environments with the purpose of induce creative thinking. I picked up this tool in grad school at The University of Kansas. I have used deductive thinking to adapt the six hats into my teamwork which I call *Creative Collaboration*. As De Bono describes, the hats can be used by one person or by an entire team. Likewise, multiple people can share the hats simultaneously, and they can exchange the hats.

In the academic environment, when I ask teams to share what some of their roles are, I typically get responses like researcher, writer, slide designer, or briefer. I call these "task focused" roles. What would similar answers sound like on your team? Maybe, secretary, marketer, engineer, salesman, all still task focused. Perfect answers, we need these roles to accomplish the mission, but how do we improve the organization? Can you think of any roles that are not "task focused"? How about, brain stormer, devil's advocate, or leader? This is how the six hats can empower initiative through creative collaboration, for **D**isabled **L**eaders.

Creative Collaboration

The first hat is the white hat. The good guy always wears the white hat, right! The white hat focuses on the facts. I consider this the role of the critical thinker. This person will check ideas for clarity, accuracy, precision, relevance, depth and breadth, logic, significance, and fairness. These areas are known as the Universal Intellectual Standards (UIS) designed by Dr. Paul and Dr. Elder.[29] The UIS are used Army-wide in nearly every education course. The white hat lives in the big box on Army Drive.

The next hat is the yellow hat. This person's role is to find the good in each idea and bring optimism to the table. I call this person Lil Miss Sunshine. He will find value in every action or idea that the group has. He will find ways to make things work and share the potential with the team. This role may seem silly to some at first, but it is extremely valuable. The yellow hat tends to set the tone for the team. Consider the value of overwhelming positivity on your team. Refusing to break. We will solve this problem and let me tell you why!

The red hat is where I sometimes lose people. It can make us uncomfortable. The red hat deals with emotions. Don't groan before you think about it. Emotions are constantly happening, changing, and evolving on your team. Our teammate, Colleen, thought she had a wonderful idea, but it was dismissed, and she felt like it was not duly considered. Now Colleen doesn't feel like a valued part of the team. She starts to check out. She decides to focus her time and efforts on other projects. Now the team has lost a valuable resource. Or perhaps another teammate is really excited about the project and has completely taken over and seems to want to do everything himself. The red hat is responsible for identifying these emotions and behaviors, and addressing them with the team as quickly as possible. It is a hard job. Essentially, this person calls production to halt. It is an important role because, if managed correctly, it will improve the end product. The quicker we can address conflict in a meaningful way, the more likely we will be able to fix and leverage it. I believe that conflict breeds creativity, but it has to be managed appropriately. My best teams have always been the ones that have figured out how to overcome adversity.

Doctors Thomas and Kilmann identify five modes of dealing with conflict in their instrument the TKI: avoiding, accommodating, competing, compromising, and collaborating.[30] Although collaborating is often considered the most valuable conflict mode, it is also thought every mode has a time and place. Yes, there are times we should avoid conflict and accommodate others. However, I consider this low-level conflict management. disabled leaders live down here. If you are always avoiding or accommodating you are not being fair to yourself or others. In my experience, it can only last so long. Eventually, the conflict will move violently into another mode, and the disabled leader will lose their opportunity to be influential. Disabled Leaders understand how to leverage each mode situationally. Yes, sometimes it is better to accommodate in order to preserve the relationship, but sometimes you have to compete for results.

The **black hat** may be the most popular of the six. This person is the teams' devil's advocate. She challenges the process, not to be a jerk, but in order to make it better. The military term for this is red teaming. The black hat asks and often attempts to answer the question, what problems or challenges might we face if we go this direction?

If you have ever seen the movie *World War Z*, you have seen a great example of what the black hat can look like. In the movie, Israel had something called the committee of ten, who is in charge of making large decisions for the country. On the committee of ten, if nine members vote one way, all agree or disagree, then it is the duty of the tenth member to vote the opposite way and discuss why. In this instance, the black hat helps us to avoid groupthink.

General Patton once said *if everybody is thinking the same way then somebody aint thinking.* It is quite easy to find teams engaged in groupthink. Someone googles a problem or suggests a solution, and the train leaves the station, with everyone on board. The thing about trains, is that they are hard to stop, nearly impossible to turn around, and they pick up steam very quickly. So, what happens when someone actually has an original, different, or better idea. Right, they get railroaded (no pun intended).

The black hat doesn't only help us think differently but can also challenge us to improve our thinking. I once worked with a retired Chief Warrant Officer. He retired from active duty in 1982, that is the year that I was born. He had been around a long time and must have been very good at his job, but no one was quite sure what his job was. At least once a week the Chief would stop into my office and start talking about Army policy, procedures, and problems. When I say problems, I mean over my head and over my paygrade problems. One day I was complaining to someone about this. He suggested that the Chief may be red teaming me, and I asked him what that was. He told me to ask the Chief the next time he stopped in. I did. The Chief mocked a shocked impression, *who me,* he asked. Then he said look, I am an old guy. I am on my way out of the Army. My experience and ideas will not mean anything. But you, you are a young buck. You are coming into the system that I have been trying to manipulate and influence for fifty years. You will have to opportunity to lead change in the Army of 2020, 2030, and 2040. So yes, some of what I bring to you may be outside of your lane, but if you are not thinking about how to fix them, who will? Wow did that ever empower me. Chief was wearing a black hat. From that day forward, I no longer dreaded Chief's visits, I looked forward to them, and even prepared for them.

The black hat is a valuable role. This role should be selected or assigned carefully, and then monitored by the blue hat. Some teammates will find challenging ideas and others a daunting task, and some will embrace it to the point of lunacy. If a team can properly leverage the black hat, then they will have an opportunity to leverage incredible initiative and imagination.

The green hat manages creativity and innovation. This role ensures that the team is actively being creative with the purpose of innovating. One activity that this person may lead is the brainstorming. When the team is brainstorming it should be capturing as many ideas as possible. Looking for quantity over quality. The first time an idea doesn't get added to the list, then the team is no longer brainstorming. The green hat ensures all ideas are being heard.

While it is great to have a brainstorming session, sometimes they may not be as productive as they could for different reasons. Some people don't like to be put on the spot. Some like to think privately before sharing publicly. It is the green hat's role to ensure that engagement during this process is maximized. One activity I like to do when brainstorming is something I call "10 ideas in 10 minutes". This could be done privately or as a team out loud. It provides structure to the session and can keep chaos from reigning, or ideas from stagnating. It also keeps the team from limiting themselves too early.

Sometimes, in a brainstorming session, we find our idea too early. The second or third idea to go on the board garners some excitement, and brainstorming stops. "10 ideas in 10 minutes" forces the group to consider more ideas and form a better screening process as they reduce the ideas which are actually viable. If you ever get to wear the green hat, have your team try this exercise, I think that you will find it productive.

There is a difference between creativity and innovation. When I encourage my students to be as creative as possible working a solution they typically agree with excitement. More often than not, the solution they derive is something I have seen a hundred times before. When I ask them, what makes their solution creative, they often point to the process, or the presentation. We have to be careful not to be blinded with creativity. While providing pretty slides may indeed take creativity, you also must ask yourself *is this useful?* I like creative slides, but I love creative ideas. Creativity may be pretty but if it isn't useful then it is not innovative.

The last hat is the blue hat. The blue hat's role is to look at the process or project holistically. In team environments, I think of the blue hat as having the team leader role.[31] In my experience, teams with four or less members typically do not have a team leader. However, teams that have more than six members must consider having a team leader. In larger teams, it can be easier for teammates to assume that others will shoulder responsibility of the task. A team leader will be in charge of ensuring that tasks and roles are fairly distributed and coordinate efforts throughout the process. The Six Thinking Hats is a great tool that aligns group tasks with group roles and keeps the entire team engaged and improving the process. The team leader would be wise to employ this model to empower initiative.

The other constraining principle of Mission Command is **Use Mission Orders**. Which is more military lingo for provide guidance. Guidance does not mean micromanage. During WWII General Patton said "Never *tell people* how to *do* things. *Tell* them what to *do* and they will surprise you with their ingenuity." See, empowerment is not a new concept, not even for the military.

Mission Orders, or guidance, can provide a certain level of structure for the purpose. In the Army, we often refer to this structure as the right and left limits. This infers flexibility within those limits. However, if for some reason you go beyond those limits, you are in danger of defeating or not meeting the purpose. Without these two constraining principles, purpose and guidance, the concept of empowerment might turn into chaos.

The final principle of Mission Command is **accept prudent risk**. Accepting risk and exercising initiative go hand in hand and are essential for empowering people. Disabled Leaders cannot empower others, or encourage initiative, without accepting some form of risk. Disabled Leaders must decide if the potential payoff is worth the possible sacrifice. That's where the prudency comes in. disabled leaders take unnecessary risks without considering a cost/benefit analysis. They see the prize and must have it no matter what the cost. Unfortunately, many times the cost is too much, bleeds the initiative, and can cause serious harm to the organization and its members.

Disabled Leaders allow their people to exercise initiative by accepting the risk for them. If the employee fails in the initiative, the Disabled Leader takes the responsibility, at least at the higher level. Disabled Leaders always take responsibility for their subordinates.

One of the biggest risks that Disabled Leaders must take is building trust. It is impossible to build trust without making yourself vulnerable. Depending on what type or how much trust you are trying to build, professional or personal, the risk can be quite costly for you or the organization, if mismanaged.

The principles of Mission Command are an excellent starting point for empowering Disabled Leaders. Disabled Leaders do not have to be military or veterans to understand or appreciate the value of these principles. That being said, these principles are not the only way to empower Disabled Leaders. While you spend a little time considering other ways to empower people, please enjoy this classic story of Mission Command in action.

Most of you have never heard of Colonel Joshua Chamberlin.[32] I consider Col. Chamberlin a phenomenal Disabled Leader who practiced Mission Command before it was even realized as a theory. Although his rank may infer that he had decades of military experience, Col.

Chamberlin commissioned into the Army as a Lieutenant Colonel during the Civil War and retired a Major General. Colonel Chamberlin was an empowering Disabled Leader and also an inspirational example of what I call Post Traumatic Success. Because of my own experiences, I believe that many veterans leverage Post Traumatic Success (PTS) as Disabled Leaders. We will discuss PTS in depth in chapter six.

Colonel Chamberlin was a college professor in Maine at the start of the Civil War. This in itself was a great accomplishment due to Chamberlin's speech impediment. He believed that the war could not be won by the north until men were willing to leave their esteemed positions in order to fight, for freedom for all. Chamberlin, being the leader that he was, led by example and took a commission in the Union Army.

Fast forward to the Battle of Gettysburg. The war was not going well for the Union at the time, and if Gettysburg fell, the capitol was likely to fall soon after. Chamberlin marched his unit over one hundred miles with little rest and no hot food. En route, his unit picked up several dozen deserters from the 2nd Maine. Instead of punishing them, and possibly shooting them, he made them aware of the situation at Gettysburg and gave them a choice to rejoin his unit or remain under guard. By talking with the men of the 2nd Maine and offering them a choice, Colonel Chamberlin built trust and empowered these men. Ultimately, the deserters decided to rejoin the Union and fight at Gettysburg.

Immediately upon arrival to Gettysburg, Colonel Strong Vincent assigned Chamberlin and his men to Little Round Top. While many junior officers did not understand the rush to the battle, only to man the back door, Vincent and Chamberlin provided the much-needed purpose. Little Round Top was the extreme left flank of the Union Army. If the confederates took that hill, they could place artillery on it, and wipe out the entire Union force. While it was tempting to take up the task on the opposite side of the hill, and assist their brother units in the fighting, the commanders were able to express the importance of holding their position, at all costs. Had the commanders not provided clear intent, the unit may have rushed to the other side of the hill to help with that fight, and we might be a very different country today.

Soon the confederates began attacking Little Round Top mercilessly. Chamberlin's unit, which had started the battle with approximately sixty rounds of ammunition per man, were down to one or two rounds. To make matters worse, the unit had sustained extreme casualties, and could no longer cover the entire flank. One more push by the confederates would completely overrun Little Round Top if Chamberlin did not do something. He didn't have much military training, but he did understand the purpose and consequences if he failed.

Chamberlin had two orders: hold the flank at all cost and do not leave the spot of the battlefield; no retreat. While that appears to be direct orders, Chamberlin found himself in a position that required him to accept prudent risk and exercise disciplined initiative. The only way, Chamberlin thought, that they could hold the flank, would be to leave their spot on the battlefield.

Chamberlin decided to lead a bayonet charge! The primary problem with this plan was that his flank no longer extended far enough. No battle drill existed for this situation. Chamberlin would have to accept risk and exercise initiative by employing creative thinking. He extended the line by thinning the flank, which weakened the line, in some spots leaving gaps. Then, once he led the charge, he ordered his company commanders to follow suit. His hope was to sweep the confederates off of the hill. He described the action to his subordinate commanders, as opening a barn door.

Chamberlin's plan worked better than he could have expected. The confederates were so surprised by a charge, that seemed to be coming from two sides, they thought that they were surrounded. Chaos ensued. Many confederates threw down their arms and either surrendered or fled the battlefield. Chamberlin had saved the Union army.

The win at Little Round Top began on the march to Gettysburg, when Chamberlin picked up the deserters. Had he not taken the time to talk with and build trust with these soldiers, he likely would have been short manned during the battle and outlasted by the confederates. His initiative and ability to accept risk on the battlefield set the conditions for victory. Creating shared understanding of purpose and intent with his subordinate commanders kept the men alive and saved the Union Army.

Colonel Chamberlin was wounded twice during the battle and would eventually die from his war wounds at the age of 85; forty-eight years later. Colonel Chamberlin was awarded the Medal of Honor for his leadership at the Battle of Gettysburg that day. Despite his disability, despite sustaining war wounds, Chamberlin was empowered to continue leading until the day that he died. He achieved the rank of Major General in the Army (Chamberlin actually presided over the surrender the Confederacy at the end of the civil war), he served as the Governor of Maine, he was appointed the President of Bowdoin College, and he was a founding member of the Maine Institution for the Blind.

It may be surprising that the Army would encourage empowerment within the agency. Pleasantly surprising. However, empowerment has become a necessity in the age of information and technology. I applaud the Army for realizing this. Now, the question becomes, can Mission Command and a hierarchal bureaucracy live in the same house? Encouraging Mission Command by deriving guiding principles is a great way to help the large organization make sense of a complex idea. Empowerment can also consist of much more.

Beyond Mission Command: CARE to Empower

It is extremely difficult to empower someone without caring. disabled leaders can hand off responsibility in the name of development, but that is not empowerment. On that note, delegation alone cannot empower. disabled leaders can say all of the right things in hopes of inspiring their people, but if they don't care, they can't empower. Theodore Roosevelt once said that people don't care how much you know until they know how much you care. The same could be said within the context of empowerment. Whether you are asking people to do things or telling them too, caring will impact the end product.

Since we know that Mission Command exists, we can surmise that this is not the only way to empower, but it is a helpful start. There are many ways that you can empower by caring. Much like the principles of Mission Command were designed to help guide the process of empowerment for military personnel, I have created a process that will encourage empowerment which I call C.A.R.E. The acronym CARE stands for **Challenge**, allow **Autonomy**, **Recognize**, and **Energize**.

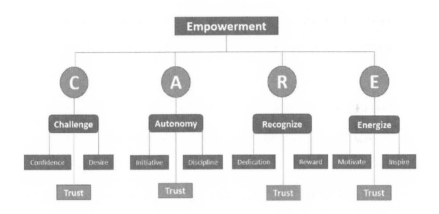

Challenge. When is the last time that you assigned someone else a task that you knew would be difficult, and take you and him out of your comfort zone? When these tasks arise, would you rather just do the job yourself in order to make sure that it gets done right and save everyone stress? What does this mean for your team? If you aren't challenging your team then you probably aren't empowering them.

There are many ways that you can challenge your team, and most of them are situational to the product or service that you provide. If you work in a customer service field, a goal may be one hundred percent customer satisfaction, but that is not a challenge. While that is a reasonable expectation, it is not empowering either. An empowering challenge must be flexible and allow for potential growth for the business and the individual. It the context of a customer service challenge, consider a broad approach. Challenge your team to try something new or different. Then, if they ask for help, begin narrowing it down. Something new, could mean a new process for assisting customers or even building relationships with them. Customer service is often the only piece of your business that the customer ever interacts with. It is important to challenge and empower the team to make corrections and improve processes when they see the gaps.

Of course, we don't all work on the front lines, or in customer service at all. So, how do Disabled Leaders challenge teams that are working on the "big project"? If you have entrusted your team with a big project, then you have probably already challenged and hopefully, empowered them. disabled leaders will often hold on to the big or important projects themselves. They either do not trust the team, they want the glory and praise, or have already overloaded the team with make work.

Disabled Leaders are not afraid to challenge the team with a big project. In fact, Disabled Leaders typically feel more confident in the success of a project when the team is involved. Nobody is as smart as everybody, right? Taking the team out of their comfort zone challenges the entire team, including the leader, to learn new knowledge, skills, and abilities. The only person that should have any real fear of failure should be the leader who assigned the task. Accepting the responsibility of failure will allow the team to explore potential within the problem and process.

Challenging the team builds confidence. It builds confidence in the leader, and confidence in the followers. As a leader, if you encourage the team to try new things and face adversity, despite difficult odds, it will build their confidence in you and they will learn to trust those behaviors. More importantly, they will be empowered to trust themselves to accept risk and achieve higher goals.

When I encounter a challenge and begin questioning myself or my team's ability, I always ask myself WWCD, What Would Charles Do? I met Charles in the Tampa VA Traumatic Brain Injury/Polytrauma Rehabilitation Program in 2004. I have met and worked with a lot of hard men in my life, but none ever came close to comparing to Charles. From the moment I met him, he had a huge smile on his face, I knew that we would be friends. I never once saw Charles not smiling. That was incredible considering his condition.

Charles was not a paraplegic and he was not vegetable, but he was something in between. Charles had taken a mortar round to the head. If you don't know what a mortar round is, go google it, then you will be impressed. No one should be able to survive such a thing. As I learned quickly though, Charles was hard headed. He survived, but now he couldn't walk or talk or anything in between. However, his limbic system was thriving!

Charles couldn't talk or write, and I couldn't hear. We were quite the pair. We loved making jokes about it to the nurses; we just knew that they were impressed with us. However, I could talk and Charles could hear just fine.

We watched football games and comedies and made fun of nurses. His family came to tolerate me pretty well. How do I know that Charles could hear and understand me? He laughed/grunted at all of my hilarious jokes.

Here is what is really so impressive about my friend Charles. Although it appeared acceptable to everyone else that he was unable to care for himself, Charles refused to accept that as fact. Anytime he needed something, it became a new challenge. Almost every time, he would fail the challenge, but it didn't stop him or even slow him down. He never called the nurse first. He needed to be able to do things for himself more than he needed things done for him. There was no shame in asking for help, but it wasn't a matter of pride, it was a matter of accepting the challenge and accomplishing something that everyone says cannot be done. There is great power in the sense of accomplishment. It is empowering.

The next time your team is working on a project and you encounter a major obstacle, what will you do? Option one, you could give up, say it can't be done, and move on to the next problem. Option two, you can pass the buck. Inform your boss that the problem cannot be solved at your level. Option three, ask for assistance from teammate, superiors, or subordinates. Or, option four, push the envelope until something gives and you either succeed or fail. The last two options are acceptable to **D**isabled **L**eaders. Sometimes we do have to ask for help, but under no circumstances does that mean that we have given up. **D**isabled **L**eaders accept many challenges on a daily basis, sometimes we win those challenges and sometimes we lose. Either way, the challenge is what empowers us to keep striving to reach our full potential.

Autonomy. I have a cousin, Steve, who has served as a police officer for just about as long as I have been doing Army things (20 years-ish). During his time on the force he has trained dozens, if not hundreds, of rookie officers. Many of these rookies are straight out of the military themselves. Steve would often rave about the rookies coming from the military as far as training, bravery, and courage are inspired. However, Steve often had one concern, these rookies always seemed to require direct orders. They had issues making decisions themselves. Obviously, this is an important trait in such a dangerous line of work. Steve once asked me, *how can I get these guys to think for themselves?*

Steve knows that he cannot be on every call with every officer. He needs to empower officers to think for themselves, make a decision, and follow through with action. We need to use autonomy to empower. A monumental difference between d̲isabled l̲eaders and **D**isabled **L**eaders is the ability and willingness to think of possible solutions and potential without relying on constant direction. Of course, it is not enough to consider the solution, **D**isabled **L**eaders take action or exercise initiative.

In this situation, how can Steve empower rookie officers to think autonomously? This example may be simpler than a corporate answer because most companies cannot provide the extensive training that rookie police officers get. Rookies receive ample training, and so one approach could be to give the young officers ambiguous problems with little guidance. Make the problems similar to issues they may face on the job. These scenarios cannot be right or wrong scenarios. The rookie must have the opportunity to be at least partially correct in whatever solution he arrives at. This should launch a discussion about how to perform better next time. Notice I said discussion, not mandate or orders. Potential shortcomings to this training may be similar to the issues that the military faces with how to empower employees in a hierarchal bureaucracy.

Experience is the best builder of autonomy and its greatest inhibitor. Experience provides opportunity to make connections and apply prior lessons to the present problem. Experience may also restrict innovative thinking; if you already know an answer, then why waste time trying to come up with something new or different. Experience must be considered delicately while approaching autonomy. While experience is the best launching point, you must not let past experience rule your thinking. Disabled Leaders understand that the way something used to work may not work now and certainly may not work best.

When Steve is training his rookies, he shares stories of his patrol experiences. His stories are not to impress the new guys, but to help them understand their training, and how it can apply. If a suspect demonstrates an action or trait that triggers the rookies' memory of the story, then he will have an opportunity to practice autonomy. The rookie may think, *does this really apply here or what could happen if I do this differently.*

In many fields, we have created policy, procedures, and regulation. Someone, somewhere along the way believes that they found a good way to do something and named it a best practice. Or, something happened that forced the organization to create a new policy restricting an action. Organizations create policy, procedures, and regulations with the best interest of the business in mind. Unfortunately, organizations could end up handicapping autonomy by creating these rules.

When is the last time that you thought of a rule or regulation as innovative? Typically, policy and procedures are intended to standardize processes. Standardization is the killer of autonomy and stagnates organizations. Most companies, in the private sector, began as an innovation, because a service or product was not being provided as well as it could be. It would be silly to think that just because you came up with a better way, it will always remain the best way. This way of thinking will eventually create an entrance for someone to do exactly what you did.

Certainly, there is a need for some regulation. However, as **D**isabled **L**eaders, we must find an appropriate balance. Policy and regulations have been kind to disabled people and have opened many doors to employment and socialization. **D**isabled **L**eaders appreciate and utilize resources, but they know that they cannot always rely on them. For example, just because the Americans with Disabilities Act (ADA) states that a public location must be accessible to handicapped patrons, doesn't mean it will be. Meet my favorite student, and **D**isabled **L**eader, Enjelokee.

Enjelokee was my student twice. Once for a direct leadership course and once for an organizational leadership course. During those two courses, or five weeks, I was both impressed and inspired by Enjelokee. Enjelokee is a senior executive for the Department of Army. Enjelokee is a **D**isabled **L**eader.

Enjelokee has cerebral palsy which severely limits his physical motor skills. Walking is a challenge, talking is a challenge, and tasks such as writing are nearly impossible. However, as Enjelokee would insist on teaching me daily, thinking and motivation were not an issue at all. Thinking and motivation are two key components of autonomy.

On the first day of the course, I was surprised by how much Enjelokee had to say and contribute to the class. On day two, I was impressed how well thought out and articulated his daily journal entry was; although it was tough to read his handwriting. On day four, I was surprised to learn that he was the team leader and primary speaker for the course project briefing. None of these tasks were easy for Enjelokee. I might equate it to assigning you to a professional basketball team and expecting you to become the team captain and lead scorer the first week. A **D**isabled **L**eader does not shy away from hard work, even when he can; instead he rises to the challenge. I imagine it may have been a challenge, convincing certain members of the team, that Enjelokee was the best person for these roles too, but he was.

Enjelokee also drove himself to class each day. In the mornings I would see him parked in the closest handicapped spots, next to our school building, which were located on the side of a street. One morning, during the second week of class, I saw him park in the handicapped spot, and then get out and begin walking (which was more of a shuffle). Instead of coming directly towards the classroom, I noticed him walking south towards another part of the school campus. I thought this was odd and wondered where he might be going. I watched him until he disappeared behind the library.

When Enjelokee arrived at the classroom that morning I greeted him and told him that I saw him earlier. Curiosity got the best of me and I asked him where he went. He said he came straight to class. I looked confused, so he clarified for me. You see, while the closest handicapped spots were located on the street next to the building, there was no access to the sidewalk. There was no ramp. Off of the street, I took for granted, that I simply stepped onto the curb and then the sidewalk. Enjelokee could not do this. He walked south, about four hundred meters, and came up the ramp there, to get to the building that was thirty feet from his car.

Enjelokee was unable to make the six-inch step onto the curb. Instead of complaining about the epic engineering fail, Enjelokee used autonomy to solve his problem. Disabled Leaders think for themselves not of themselves. It would have been very easy to complain and lay blame for the oversight on the Army, but how would that have helped Enjelokee? He still had to get from his car to the building. Even if the Army agreed to fix the problem, it would take a year or two. Welcome to the Army. Despite the difficulty of shuffling an extra eight hundred meters to get to his class, Enjelokee knew this was his best option, and owned it.

How many times have you or your team hit a hurdle or a barrier? It may have seemed unsurmountable, impossible to overcome, or just an inconvenience. What did you do? disabled leaders will quickly decide something is impossible, and because of the challenge, that it is no longer their problem. If they would take the time and dedication to practice autonomy, most problems can be solved, one way or another, although it will likely mean more work for you.

Above I mentioned that two key components of autonomy are thinking and motivation. We discussed thinking critically and creatively in earlier sections.

Sometimes, good ideas are immediate, and I believe in going with your gut. No matter how quickly the good idea comes, Disabled Leaders carefully examine the potential. Allowing autonomy takes time and motivation. Disabled Leaders are motivated to think for themselves and become more motivated when their ideas get derailed by the unforeseen challenges.

Enjelokee faces a plethora of day to day challenges. I doubt that his supervisor expected him to volunteer to travel across country for five weeks of leadership training, but he did. Given Enjelokees' exceptional challenges, he probably could have gotten a pass on some of the requirements in these courses: daily journals, public briefing, leadership philosophy. I saw him typing his one-thousand-word leadership philosophy in class one afternoon at the rate of maybe five words per minute. Disabled Leaders exceed expectations through empowerment. They have been empowered and continue to empower themselves. Thinking for themselves means believing in themselves. I believe that Enjelokee will accomplish anything that he wants too; will you?

Enjelokee inspired me with his initiative so much, that the second time he came for training, I knew I had to do something for him. The Army had still not fixed the problem of the curb versus the sign, so I took it upon myself to help. I built a little wooden ramp at home and put it next to the handicapped parking spot. Enjelokee laughed at my craftsmanship, but I think he really appreciated it. About two years after submitting my initial complaint/concern about the situation, the Army finally implemented a solution. Instead of putting in a ramp, they replaced the handicapped parking signs with "No Parking" signs. In this scenario, did the Army employ **D**isabled **L**eadership or d̲isabled l̲eadership? My advice to the Army is that **D**isabled **L**eadership is more than lip service and meeting regulations.

Recognize. Every day, our teams show up, give one hundred percent, and do great work. Ok, well, maybe not every day. Empowered teams led by **D**isabled **L**eaders are tremendously productive though. As **D**isabled **L**eaders, we now understand that empowering our team is not a one and done deal, and that empowerment is on-going. Every success and every failure should be recognized, for different reasons. There are other drivers that **D**isabled **L**eaders must recognize to maintain an empowered team too, including many of the topics which have been discussed previously in this book. A few of concepts that have been reoccurring throughout this book, that are important to recognize, are desire, dedication, and discipline. The Three D's of Disabled Leadership. Contain your excitement until the next chapter.

Let's start with the obvious; recognizing success. It seems like common sense that **D**isabled **L**eaders should acknowledge and celebrate the big wins. However, you might be surprised how often disabled leaders overlook this obvious opportunity to empower the team. Two reasons disabled leaders ignore accomplishments are indifference and to infringe.

Some disabled leaders simply do not care about their teams, and therefore they are indifferent. They believe that the only reward or recognition for doing your job should be your paycheck. Maybe there is some truth to this philosophy, but remember, you get what you pay for. For many **D**isabled **L**eaders, recognition does not need to be in the form of a bonus or a raise. Teams are often empowered by intrinsic motivations, and they will thrive if recognized. Unfortunately, some disabled leaders do not understand the value of even verbally recognizing the team for a job well done. For many disabled leaders refusing recognition is unintentional.

Infringement is intentional. disabled leaders, who refuse to recognize good work completed by the team, because they either want to take credit for the work or are afraid of the team's success, will infringe or undermine the team success. Either of these cases are ingredients for a toxic work environment. Eventually, the team will catch on to what is happening, and it will negatively impact performance. Disabled Leaders understand that giving the team credit that it is due and recognizing the team's success will empower everyone involved; including themselves. When the team performs well and looks good, so does the leader, and the organization benefits.

Recognizing success can be difficult and frustrating. Wanting to recognize your team and being able to, are very different things. Consider a team who has just achieved an initiative that is forecasted to bring the company $10M. The Disabled Leader wants to recognize the teams good work, in order to empower the next initiative, by giving each team member a $5,000 bonus. She submits the request to higher headquarters and it is denied. Would it be more empowering to tell the team what she tried to do for them, or to not tell them, and find a way to recognize the team that is suitable to headquarters? Telling the team may help them trust or like her more, but would it empower them? Why make corporate $10M if they don't appreciate it enough to allow me to keep a small piece of what I made?

Empowering teams through recognition requires extreme finesse. If one person appears to be getting recognized far more than the rest of the team, then you may need to ask yourself or the team, why? Is the individual really outperforming the rest of the team, is there a bias, or are you missing pertinent information? Unfair recognition could lead to resentment within the team and inadvertently cause conflict.

Energize. Empowerment requires energy. Half of my readers just cringed. On the surface it may seem like empowering your team makes your job easy. If you still believe that, then I encourage you to go back and re-read the first fifty pages of this chapter. Empowerment is not easy, it takes time, and it takes effort.

Let's take a paragraph or two to consider the complexities of the process of empowerment, and realize the energy required, from start to finish. We have already screwed up, because to empower means there should be no finish or end. Empowerment is an all or nothing proposition. You cannot empower the team one week and the next expect them to conform to some conflicting expectation; it won't end well. So, once you make the decision to empower your team, you have to see it through. If you make the decision to stop, for some reason empowerment just isn't working, you had better be certain, because you will never be able to empower that team again.

You understand the implications and you are certain that you want to empower your team, great, let's do this thing. Because you have bought into the Disabled Leader culture, you decide to use the C.A.R.E. model to empower your team. You are brainstorming all of the ways that you intend to challenge the team and allow autonomy, but now you have some concern. If you give the team all of this power, what role do you play, where is your power? As an empowering manager, you will spend most of your time asking two questions: what do you need from me and how can I help? Your job is to provide support and acquire the team the resources they need to be successful. That should keep you busy for a while.

You are probably realizing, like the military, that you should incorporate some limits, so that empowerment doesn't turn into chaos. Man, you're getting good! Now that your job security is back, you can figure out exactly how much authority and decisionmaking you should grant to your team. How many hours do you think you have spent on this empowerment initiative so far? Take that number and double it. That is just to get started.

Managing an empowered team requires incredible diplomacy. If you reject too many ideas or step on too many toes, the team will lose their sense of empowerment. There is nothing less effective than a team that is supposed to be running on empowerment but is not. A high level of shared understanding, and patience to allow the process to run its course, will be instrumental to effectively empowering your team. So, when I warn you that empowering takes energy, I mean it takes physical energy and emotional energy.

Of course, the payoff for your investment of energy can be enormous. Not only should you have improved product results, but your processes will become simpler and more productive as well. Perhaps most importantly, an empowered team will become an energized team. An energized team can be an unstoppable force to be reckoned with. Energized teams are the game changers in industries and the conquer of giants.

Many of today's managers grew up watching innovative companies such as Apple Inc. and Amazon disrupt markets and conquer gigantic corporations such as IBM or Wal-Mart. While it is easy to credit these company's successes to individuals like Steve Jobs and Jeff Bezos, we know as they know, that they are successful because of their teams.

Start-ups have a unique ability to energize their teams long term. When an organization or team forms under the philosophy of empowerment, it has the capability to carry the team longer and further than a team that tries to implement a strategy of empowerment later. For example, if a team is struggling and the leader decides to implement an empowerment initiative, the team may have doubt in the back of their mind. *What will REALLY happen if I do that? Why is this happening now? How long will this last? If this doesn't work, what will happen to the team?* It is far tougher to become empowered in an environment that has never exercised that level of trust before. However, the team that trusts first, and forms with empowerment, has the capability to sustain a high level of energy for an extended period of time.

Energy, through empowerment, is a big part of what will bring results. My mentor, Delford Smith, whom I have mentioned previously and will again before the end of this book, liked to say *when you're building your team you should look for three qualities in each individual 1. Integrity 2. Intelligence 3. Energy.* If anyone of those three are lacking, the other two will cause you problems. For example, if you hire someone who is smart and capable but lacks integrity, you are going to get the wrong end of that stick eventually. What Del didn't tell me, but helped me learn, was that the team's energy is primarily a result of the culture the leader builds. A culture of trust and empowerment will breed energy, and energy will drive success.

C.A.R.E is the four-step process discussed above that you can use to empower your team. Ultimately, it is your team, so you must figure out what will work to empower them. Every team is different and there is no magic answer for empowerment, but I believe this is a good starting point. Above I mentioned that it is far tougher to incorporate empowerment into an existing team than empowering a new team. I hold that as a true. However, by no means does that infer that existing teams cannot be empowered, it will just take more work.

Just as **D**isabled **L**eaders have been empowered to succeed in their lives, they empower teams to succeed in their work. disabled leaders tend to lack trust in their teams and micro manage them, often taking credit for successes and blaming failure. When managers learn to C.A.R.E. they can empower their teams to become **D**isabled **L**eaders.

The Three D's of Disabled Leadership

In the previous chapter I got you all excited about the Three D's of Disabled Leadership, and now I have to deliver on that, I guess. The three D's are the pillars which elevate and empower Disabled Leadership. These pillars are built from a foundation of resilience. The pillars maximize use of resilience and empowerment to achieve Disabled Leadership. The Three D's of Disabled Leadership are Desire, Dedication, and Discipline.

Desire

Have you ever wanted something? Like really bad? No, like really, really bad?! Did anyone tell you that you couldn't have it? Insist that it wasn't possible? Did you get it? What did you do to get it? Did you have to overcome any challenges? Clear any hurdles? Overcome any obstacles? Once you got what you wanted, was it was worth it? How did you feel about the accomplishment?

Nothing motivates like desire does. It doesn't matter whether the motives are intrinsic or extrinsic.[33] If you want an education, you will get it. If you want to be rich, you will find a way. If you want to walk again, you will do everything within your power to be successful. The catch is, you must have a real desire.

Desire is more than a wish.[34] You can't just decide that you want to be a pilot one day and expect someone to hand you a license and a job simply because you want it. That should be obvious. You have to work hard and fight for what you want. Whether your desire is to be a millionaire or acquire basic equal opportunity and rights, you are going to have to work for it, and you will probably need help.

Almost one hundred years ago, in 1920, the amendment for the Women's Right to Vote was passed.[35]

In 1964, segregation ended with the Civil Rights Act.[36] Not until 1990 did the Americans with Disabilities Act pass.[37] In 2015, same sex couples were allowed to marry by federal law.[38] In 2018, I have marched with fathers from all over the U.S. for equal parenting rights.[39] What drove all of these movements? Desire! Desire to be treated equally and fairly.

We can easily accept that all of these folks desired those things now; in hindsight. However, you could never convince me that women didn't want voting rights for 244 years, blacks wanted slavery and segregation, disabled people didn't want education or jobs, it's true that homosexuals always wanted to marry, and fathers certainly deserve equal rights in raising their children. The desire existed, and it still exists. It doesn't seem like these are things that we should have to work for, but they are. If desire can defeat policy and law, I'm telling you, it can achieve anything.

Unless you, by chance, just opened this book to this page, you have already read several stories of how Disabled Leaders leveraged desire to accomplish their goals. In this section I would rather encourage you to consider your own desires. What is something that you want to accomplish? What is standing in your way? How can you overcome these obstacles? What purpose will achieving this goal serve? Once you accomplish this goal what is next? Take some time here to consider your goals? Why did you pick up this book?

Desire is powerful. It must be considered thoroughly and acted upon carefully. If you decide that you want to go to college, ask yourself why. What is the desire behind the goal? If the desire is to make more money, then there may be other options for you than going into debt with student loans or not sleeping for four years. More importantly, if your desire is not actually to get an education, there is a reasonable chance that you may fail. If your desire is to be a veterinarian, then you know that school is a requirement. The ends justify the means. The only way to become a veterinarian is by going to veterinarian school. Getting an education is not the only way to make more money. Once you realize that there are other ways to attain your desire, there is a risk of abandoning the initial goal for an easier or different path.

Desire is a meaningful starting point. As we have figured out, desire cannot carry you across the finish line, but will give you a push when you need it. Once you have identified true desire, the next step to success will be dedication.

Dedication

Desire without dedication will be fruitless. Desire provides a goal, but dedication will make it real. The desire does not become tangible until you start to do something about it. To make a desire a reality you must dedicate yourself, time, and resources. Dedicating yourself is the most difficult, dedicating your time infers commitment, and investing resources promises a return on investment.

What is something that you have dedicated yourself too? Physical fitness, dieting, or fundraising for a cause all require dedication, but do they necessitate "dedicating yourself"? Perhaps, at least partially. I mean, physical fitness is an hour a day, dieting is difficult but is typically short term, and promoting a cause is rewarding but generally sporadic. Can you think of something that required your dedication for a majority of the day, for an extended period of time? Perhaps raising a child, creating financial independence, a start-up business, or even perhaps learning to walk again. There are plenty of things that we dedicate ourselves too. I don't mean to minimize anyone's dedication, but I am asking you to question it. How dedicated are you to your goal? Could you improve your dedication?

Dedicating yourself requires unwavering commitment and relentless willpower. When things are going well, you can't get comfortable. Comfort can cause complacency. Complacency can cause a collapse or even a crash. When things are going badly, you must remain focused. Everyone has set backs in every endeavor. Even the most successful people experience setbacks. Remember, Steve Jobs was fired from his own company, but was eventually asked to return, and he changed the world. The bad usually isn't as terrible as it may seem initially and is unlikely unsurmountable. Dedication requires constant courage to continue. There will be times when you will want to quit, it may even be the most logical choice. Other people will tell you to quit while you're ahead. There are always a million reasons to give up, but in these times of doubt, desire and dedication will serve to help you persevere.

I have mentioned my mentor a couple of times already, but now I feel that the time is right to tell you more about him. Delford Michael Smith (DMS) was the founder and owner of Evergreen Aviation for almost sixty years before passing away in 2014. DMS was a **D**isabled **L**eader for many reasons including desire and dedication.

DMS lived in an orphanage as a young child. He was eventually adopted; however, a few months later his adopted father passed away. DMS found odd jobs to contribute means for he and his adoptive mother to survive. He obtained a $.50 loan from a bank and bought a lawn mower, which allowed him to earn enough money to buy a home for them to live in, when he was 12 years old. His initiative was instrumental to their survival, and built confidence for future potential ventures.

As a young man, DMS served a tour of duty in Korea. During this time, he found his passion for helicopters. He applied and tried everything he could to fly helicopters for the military. Unfortunately, he was rejected from pilot training because DMS was color blind. Although DMS loved the military, he knew his calling was in the sky, and he had an unwavering desire to fly.

DMS dedicated himself, and became a pilot. A few years later he took initiative and bought his own helicopter. It wasn't long before he owned a fleet of helicopters which he often referred to as "workhorses" and "angels of mercy". DMS pioneered many of today's common uses for helicopters including industrial logging and firefighting. Over the next fifty years DMS diversified his company, which was now called Evergreen International Aviation, to consist of eleven sister companies and a world class aviation museum campus. When I worked for the helicopter company it had over one hundred aircraft under contract, and the fixed wing company was operating thirteen 747s. DMS' accomplishments were nothing short of remarkable. How did this orphan boy transition from a $.50 loan to a billionaire?

Most incredible stories such as DMS' are born from passion, but what is the relationship between passion and desire? DMS had a passion for flying, but he also had a desire to learn to fly. The passion is your purpose, and desire is the motivation to achieve the purpose. The gap between the two is where dedication comes in.

DMS had a passion for flying, not just piloting. Piloting was a means to an end. Sure, it took dedication to overcome his disability, and become a pilot, but he had the discipline not to stop there. DMS realized that he was capable of much more than being a pilot. He saw possibilities that others hadn't. His passion for flying became a desire to fly himself, and through discipline, he revolutionized an industry. To learn more about DMS' incredible life, I encourage you to read *The Evergreen Story by Bill Yenne.* DMS was an inspiring **D**isabled **L**eader and the most caring mentor I have ever had; this is my tribute.

Discipline

One of the first things that DMS ever said to me, that stuck with me, was that the military instilled the discipline in me that was required to be successful. I believe that is true. Not only did the military provide me with experiences, but it taught me priorities. We worked hard and we played hard, but the work always got done first.

While some people can appreciate this message, for the majority, it may be incomprehensible, since less than one percent of Americans have served in the Armed Forces. We appreciate their service, but I am not implying that veterans are so special, as to be the only folks who understand, and utilize discipline. Millions have honed and reinforced their behaviors to achieve almost any goal that you can think of, but in my opinion, **D**isabled **L**eaders are the most inspirational and impactful.

Perhaps someone with dyslexia is reading this sentence; that's discipline. It's hard. He doesn't want to do it. He reads anyway. He knows that he will never completely overcome dyslexia, but by having the discipline to try, he is not letting dyslexia defeat him. He could probably get his books on audio, but that could be considered accepting defeat. So, he maintains the discipline required to struggle through line after line and page after page. Now he reaps the benefits that life tried to elude him. As a result of reading, he gains mental stimulation, memory improvement, knowledge, and a plethora of other benefits. If he were not disciplined in his dedication, he might be far less likely to achieve his desired results.

That was more D's than you bargained for. Desire, dedication, and discipline are necessary pillars to becoming a **D**isabled **L**eader. If any one of the three are lacking, you will have a rough time accomplishing your goals, and it is likely that everything will come crashing down on you. Although we have discussed many other traits and behaviors that **D**isabled **L**eaders emulate, these three pillars must be included for successful longevity. You may not start here, but if you are to be successful, you will end up here, at some point.

Disabled Leaders Demonstrate Resilience

It was quite difficult to come this far, and write this much, without a rant on resilience. I know it was obvious, and there are a million places throughout this book that I could have analyzed resilience, but I also knew that this topic was so huge to my theory, that it needed its own chapter. Without a doubt resilience is the primary attribute that sets Disabled Leaders apart and ahead of everyone else.

Simply put, resilience is the ability to bounce back when something bad happens or the ability to overcome an overwhelming challenge.[40] Of course, easily said is not easily done. How do Disabled Leaders exhibit such resilience while disabled leaders struggle and often fail? The textbook answers are probably things like nature versus nurture or fight versus flight. Let's explore this concept without the psychology books though.

There is a popular story of a professor who stood in front of his class holding a small glass of water. He asked the class how much they thought the glass weighed. After a few guesses the professor tells the class that they have missed the point; it doesn't matter how much the glass of water weighs at that moment in time. What matters is how long he holds on to it. If he only held it for a few minutes the weight would be inconsequential. If he held it for a few hours, his arm would probably get sore or begin to cramp. If he held onto it for days he would most likely be in considerable pain. The lesson is to learn when to let things go. Again, that is easier said than done. So, how do we know when it is time to let things go? More importantly, how do we let things go? How can we change ourselves? To begin answering these questions, let's look at a couple of case studies and analyze how Disabled Leaders are able to conquer obstacles that disabled leaders cannot.

Disabled Leaders are not perfect. Sometimes they exhibit disabled leadership. It happens to the best of us. The Americans with Disabilities Act (ADA) classifies some drug addictions as a disability. Before we jump to conclusions, this is not referring to the casual marijuana user or the guy who likes to have a beer after work, and although I would consider vaping a disability, the ADA does not. (insert LOL emoji) The addiction must pose a substantial limitation to one or more major life activities to be considered a disability. According to the ADA, major life activities include: caring for oneself, performing manual tasks, seeing, hearing, eating, sleeping, walking, standing, lifting, bending, speaking, breathing, learning, reading, concentrating, thinking, communicating, and working. Whether you consider addiction a choice or a disease, it can create a terrible handicap for the individual.

I have seen addiction disable warriors whom I once believed to be gods amongst men. Society sees the homeless heroin addict curled up in the alleyway and labels him a dirtbag. In reality, that dirtbag is a forgotten hero. A soldier who answered his country's call, a Ranger, a wounded warrior. His own government began shoving drugs into his body before he even deployed. He lived on IV drips for weeks at a time, on a mountain that no opposing force had been on since Alexander the Great. Some missions lasted for days on end without sleep, during which time he was fed drugs the equivalent of speed. When he got scraped and bruised and beat up on missions he was given dangerous amounts of pain pills and told to drive on. For the more serious injuries they gave him "lollipops," which is morphine, while still in a combat zone; while using a weapon. The opium used in the lollipops may have originated from the very field that he walked through to reach the battlefield. It is not difficult to figure out *where* his addictions originated or how they formed.

And then, the beginning of the end. On his seventh combat deployment he took a Rocket Propelled Grenade (RPG) to the abdomen. He should have died, but not yet. First, he lost three quarters of his stomach. The pain was nearly unbearable. The drugs help. His wife and child visit as often as possible, but the bills have piled up, mommy has to work, and baby girl has to go to school. The stress builds. His wife watches her loves transformation into something, someone that she doesn't recognize.

A year passes, then another. He is home now; medically retired. He still can't do much, the pain slows him down too much. The drugs make him constantly irritable. The family fights, a lot, over silly things, finances, and responsibilities. His wife finally reaches her breaking point, for whatever reason, and takes his daughter and leaves him. Family court awards her alimony and child support based on his disability income. Suddenly he has lost all means and all hope. The same person we called a war hero two years ago is now a "dirtbag" "drug addict" "deadbeat dad". Where did he fail? At what point should resilience have kicked in? Why didn't it? Where did WE fail?

We start to understand the complexities of overcoming tragedies by using empathy. What would I do if I were in his shoes? Where did the trouble really begin? Honestly, was this fate, or is there anything he could have done to fix his issues? When should he have recognized his dependency on drugs? Should the medics and doctors have identified the addiction and used alternative medicine? Is it someone else's responsibility to ensure his safety? What about the wife, what should she have done? Should she be held responsible in any way for his undoing?

This is a true story. It's one story. There are tens of thousands more like it from the Global War of Terrorism alone. For every tragic situation, that often seems by design, there is an equally inspiring story of someone who overcame all of this madness, to achieve greatness. What is the difference? Where did the paths diverge? Why did the paths diverge? Why do I keep asking all of these absurd questions?!

Remember, we are trying not to use pop psychology to answer our questions. In reality, I don't think that we need to open any other books, we already have the right book open. Resilience has to begin with self-awareness, just as this book did. You have to know what is going on with you. Be able to recognize that something has changed. Something is impacting your performance or behavior. Yes, the mission is important but never as important as your health. I am not sure that social awareness would be particularly helpful in this instance as the government tends to mask their intentions well.

Hindsight is 20/20 but let's look back and try to identify instances in the scenario where adequate self-awareness may have changed the outcome for this Ranger:

1. Perhaps this Ranger was doing his duty or maybe he was an adrenaline junkie. Seven Ranger combat deployments is intense. At some point the

Disabled Leader has to ask himself if he has done enough. The mental and physical toll of pushing oneself to the limit, repeatedly, can easily cripple even the strongest leader.

2. Excessive injuries should have probably been a red flag to the Ranger, his medical personnel, and leadership team. It either indicated that he was pushing too hard, or creating intentional injuries for either drugs or maybe for attention.

3. Requesting or relying on excessive medications. Being severely wounded in action and needing medicine for survival is one thing, but building a reliance on drugs due to excessive injuries is another. The body most likely built up a tolerance to the pain killers he was already taking, forcing the medical staff to give him increased doses to save his life. The increased doses worsened his addiction or need for the drug.

4. The one aspect I am sure of, is that strong doses of pain killers can make even the nicest guy a jerk. I personally have had to take drugs such as Percocet and Vicodin in the past, and my friends and family told me later that I was a complete asshole while

on them. I didn't even realize I was behaving differently. Now I try to imagine living on them, needing these drugs daily, for an extended period of time. If we look up oxycodone side effects it does not say anything about behavior, although it does list death as a side effect. If we cannot assess our behaviors or research the appropriate side effects of the drug, how can we be self-aware. It's a difficult situation that can possibly be improved by simply asking close ones for feedback on our actions and behaviors. disabled leaders are uncomfortable with honest feedback and will dismiss the notion of its relevance and effectiveness. Disabled Leaders value other's perspectives, and use the opportunity to change. In this scenario, that change may have saved this Ranger.

5. When his family (wife) abandoned him, that should have been the final wake up call. Ok, this is serious. Maybe it was too late for her, maybe it was too late for their marriage, but it wasn't too late for him. If he had not asked for the right kind of help up to this point, now was the time. If the

wife was unwilling to help, find a friend, go home to your immediate or extended family, go to the Veterans Affairs, or reach out to your military friends. Quite often your Ranger buddy has a better idea of what you have been through and what you are going through, and they will give you a no BS assessment of what they see. We tend to respect and accept the opinions of our brothers and sisters in arms, who have shared our experiences, more than civilians. Together you can figure out your next step to get back on the right path. The point is, chances are far better for success if you are actively looking for help.

I am sure that there were many more opportunities to turn things around, and I am sure that there many other challenges that no one will ever be aware of. It's hard to judge a situation like this, and I certainly do not want to try. I simply want to help others help themselves. No matter how bad the situation seems there are always things that we can do to improve our circumstances, and our chances of survival and success. That isn't coming from some snot nosed ivy league academic. I have had and continue to have my share of challenges. From being left on a doorstep as a child, a subpar primary education, being severely wounded in action, or even having a corrupt court system tell me that I cannot raise my children and can only see them a few times a year if I pay an excessive extortion rate (google social security act title 4 D&E). We all have our own issues and we have to fight our own fights, but how?

Self-awareness is always the best launching point. Having a strategy or a plan in place for when life gets rough can help us keep perspective on the true significance of the problem, and what is really important. I have created what I refer to as The Ranger Resiliency Model, easier remembered as the FAN, that I use to guide myself through troubled waters, and keep me calm. Hopefully these concepts may be useful to you as well in achieving resiliency.

F.A.N.

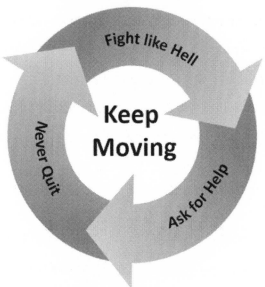

The Ranger Resiliency Model

1. **Fight like Hell.** First things first, never stop fighting. Fight with fierceness, and with certainty that you will not lose. Most problems in life that I apply these rules to are worth fighting for. Self-preservation, family and friends, and equal rights are great examples of things to fight for. Those are general examples, but what are some specific things that you are willing to fight or have fought for?

Once the fight starts, you must see it through, even if you lose. There will be times when the fight isn't going well, and you may want to quit. I will tell you now, quitting is NOT an option. If you are tired, take a rest, but do not give up, ever. Even when it appears you may lose badly, most often, some good will come from the fight. The good may not impact you directly, but it may make the next persons fight that much easier. Your fight will serve as others inspiration.

Fighting for what we believe in changes the situation. If gives us a certain amount of control that we wouldn't have if we chose not to fight. Consider cancer patients who have a "kick cancers ass" attitude have a significantly higher recovery rate than patients whom simply quietly seek treatment. Blogs, marathons, and pink ribbons improve not only awareness and funding, but the patient's attitude, and desire for survival. As we know, desire is an unstoppable force. Of course, these success stories also inspire others to fight. What fight will you inspire?

2. **Ask for Help.** Asking for help can be hard. So many things get in the way: egos, time, escalation, defeat, and much more. While there is honor in fighting your own fight, there is no shame in asking for help. Everyone needs help from time to time.

   I encourage you to be proactive. Ask for help early, before things become dire. Try to avoid being reactive and waiting until help is the last resort. If help is the last resort, you still have to ask, things may just be more difficult than if you had asked earlier.

   Do not be embarrassed to ask for help. Asking for help is a sign of strength. Let me say this again but differently, asking for help IS NOT a sign of weakness. Whether you need help with your wheel chair, writing a dissertation, or even psychological support there is someone willing to help. Assistance is the reason family, friends, and entire organizations exist. Some of the most successful people I know would not have achieved anything without help.

   I also encourage you to offer help every chance you get. What harm could it do? How often do you say something like *lemme know if you need any help,* or where I come from *just holler if you need a hand?* Offering help should be more than a courtesy or politeness. I hear people say those phrases dozens of times a day, usually as they are walking away. I wonder, when is the last time they followed up?

Have you ever helped someone without asking? What were the results? It can be quite powerful, but it can also blow up in your face. This is how social awareness comes into play. What could happen if I help versus what could happen if I don't help? Does the good outweigh the bad? Would the person you are helping see it the same way? Obviously, in life or death situations, most of the time, you should help. However, when you see someone really struggling with something, they tell you they don't want your help, but you help anyway, it could hurt. You may have just stolen their sense of accomplishment or empowerment. Awareness or understanding of the assistance needed is going to be essential in ensuring the person isn't afraid to ask for help the next time.

3. **Never Quit.** You can't lose if you never quit. Even if you think you're losing or have lost, as long as you keep moving, keep working, keep trying, keep learning, eventually you will succeed. The ONLY way that you can truly lose in the long run is by quitting.

    I notice that many people are averse to failure, but not to quitting. When times get hard it is easy to say *it can't be done* and just quit. This easy out lets us believe that we have not failed and places the blame elsewhere. Let's call it what it is, quitting is failing by failure. Failing by failure insinuates one has primarily failed himself, typically by not rising to the challenge.

    What about the phrase quitting while you are ahead? Ok, that may be relevant in gambling, but in most other cases, it is an excuse. It means that you are unwilling to accept the risk or take the initiative required to continue. Some would say the risk isn't worth it, but I believe it is always worth the risk not to be a quitter. If something needs to change, then by all means, alter your approach, but risk and change do not warrant quitting...and it never will.

In the beginning of this chapter I shared a quick analogy about letting things go. If letting things go is essential to resilience, then why can't I quit? Quitting and letting things go are not synonymous. Letting things go does not mean that you are quitting. Letting go refers to harboring hate, resentment, or ill will towards ourselves or others that may keep us from achieving our goals. We have to let go of the emotions that hold us back, and do not allow us to focus on the desired end state. Too often we are defeated by our emotions, and not the real issue. Letting go keeps us from quitting.

The Ranger Resiliency Model is a simple and hopefully effective way to remember to Keep Moving. Three easy reminders of how tough we really are. For our "strong rangers" out there, who's ranger buddy is reading this to them, if you think you might have trouble remembering the model, the acronym F.A.N. might help.

What do we use fans for? To cool off! Ok, I have officially taken this too far.

In chapter four I mention Post Traumatic Success which of course is an adaption from Post-Traumatic Stress Disorder (PTSD). While PTSD has been a serious and escalating concern for the military over the past few decades, PTSD does not only affect military personnel. Civilian Trauma and Combat Trauma share many of the same symptoms. Civilian Trauma can be caused by events such as assault and accidents. There are many cases of job-related PTSD in the private sector as well. While military PTSD can be caused by direct action, much of it is caused by similar events as Civilian Trauma. Hundreds of thousands of people in the U.S. suffer from PTSD, but the more we learn, the easier it is to manage. Resiliency bridges the gap between PTSD and Post Traumatic Success.

As **D**isabled **L**eaders learn to master resiliency everything seems to become clearer and easier. **D**isabled **L**eaders accept the things that have happened to them and manage the courage to live with them the best that they can. Making peace with your Post Traumatic Stress is by no means as easy as I make it sound, but it is necessary. Dr. Fredrike Bannink, who leads research into Post Traumatic Success, states that it *helps make the victim better instead of bitter.*

I am not a clinical psychologist, and therefore I do not feel qualified to tell you how to make peace with your PTSD. I do however very much like the idea of Post Traumatic Success (PTS) though. PTS absolutely requires masterful resiliency skills and behaviors. The sheer power in the concept of PTS is enough to inspire many victims to become **D**isabled **L**eaders as you learn to turn your weakness into strength.

In my mind, PTS does not only refer to assault and accident victims. Any person who has been handicapped or disabled physically and mentally can achieve PTS. Any handicap is capable of being traumatic. The ability to overcome or completely expunge the "disorder" part of PTSD is incredibly empowering. Of course, getting rid of that stress is far easier for some than others. Replacing stress with success allows **D**isabled **L**eaders the opportunity to influence and inspire other victims.

No matter what our disabilities are, no matter how society encourages us to take the easy path, Disabled Leaders are still capable of forging their own destiny. Resiliency leads to PTS by insisting that we challenge ourselves. An example might be, being told that you will never walk again, and given a wheel chair, but deciding not to resign your future so easily. Surviving itself is not acceptable. Disabled Leaders can achieve anything, perhaps even more than we could have before our life changing event. Resiliency insists to us that we must accomplish more. It is not that we have to prove something to others, its more about what we can prove to ourselves. We can and we will.

PTS sounds great, but where do I begin? What does PTS look and feel like? How do I know if I am achieving PTS? Great questions guys let's attempt to answer them.

Well, we have been discussing the starting point; resiliency. PTS begins when you decide that you are not going to let an accident, assault, or some other life changing event define you. You accept resiliency and promise yourself to 1. Fight like Hell 2. Ask for Help 3.

Never Quit. In doing these three things, no matter what the context, you are challenging yourself. Challenging yourself to be better than you were, better than you are, and better than current expectations. Accepting the challenge requires desire. Accomplishing the challenge requires dedication. Overcoming the challenges within the challenge requires discipline. All three of these require resiliency. Resiliency is the **D**isabled **L**eaders Alpha and Omega. Nothing else will work without it.

Your approach is working! Resiliency is paying off and you begin to see results. What should you expect? Success breeds success. When you begin to see the change and value in one aspect of your life, your desire will shift to improve the other parts as well. Consider the adult with dyslexia who decides to power through using difficult techniques and strategies he learns to read. Imagine the feeling of accomplishment. This handicap has been hanging over his head his entire life, but now he has accomplished what he once thought could not be done. The sky is the limit. Maybe now he will go back and finish high school, or even go to college. Maybe he will finally start writing the novel that has been marinating in his brain for ten years. Once the ball is rolling it won't stop unless you stop it, and why would you do that?!

Within the initial success, your entire perspective can change instantaneously. At first it may just be a glimmer of hope. Things that you have always thought to be impossible begin to seem conceivable. With each victory you will build confidence in yourself and your abilities. There will be set backs of course, but by this point you are well aware of how to overcome those using FAN. With a few victories under your belt you will come to realize that nothing is impossible. Disabled Leaders can accomplish anything.

Once you have achieved PTS, your expectations of yourself change dramatically. Your expectations of others change too. Perhaps you used to rely on others for assistance with something that was difficult due to your disability, but now you realize that you can do it for yourself with a little more dedication and discipline. Now you wouldn't expect others to try to help you with that task, unless you ask. You also may expect others to challenge themselves more. If they are doubting themselves, then there is your opportunity to inspire them with your experiences and accomplishments. Don't be smug, but proceed with the attitude that if you can do that then they can do this, but it won't be easy. As always, don't forget to offer to help!

Overcoming tragedy, instilling hope and confidence, and building and sharing success is what PTS encompasses. Each of those steps require resiliency. Hopefully you are currently working on your own PTS. I will share my most proud PTS.

Way back in the beginning of this book I told you that I barely graduated high school. That wasn't a joke. I read two books during my entire stint in high school, both were by S.E. Hinton. Rarely did I even read the text books. I would skim them at best and convince myself that I had read them. No one bothered correcting me. The next book I read, Memnoch the Devil by Anne Rice, was when I was twenty years old pulling guard duty in Afghanistan. Someone had left it sitting on the guard vehicle. I was surprised by how much I enjoyed it, but did not make plans to read anymore of her work. I read her book simply to pass time.

I had handicapped myself long before I became disabled. Many of us do, without even realizing it. That statement isn't only referring to reading, or even learning. We are all capable of accomplishing much more than we often allow ourselves. I didn't believe that reading served any purpose other than perhaps entertainment, and maybe I really didn't believe in me.

Then I incurred a disability in 2004. I not only lost my hearing, but I lost the capability of doing many things that I could do before. Simple things and silly things. I couldn't listen to music or even really have a decent conversation. I also had to re-tune basic motor functions, and learned to walk and swim again. In the chaos of learning how to live again my disability helped me to overcome my handicap.

Being deaf meant I could no longer rely on the easiest way of communicating and receiving information. For over a year, every person who wanted to tell me something had to write it down. Even once I received the Cochlear Implant, communication in day to day settings is extremely challenging. My disability was forcing me out of my comfort zone.

Now, instead of relaxing and watching television or a movie I had to read closed captions. It was hard, really hard, at first. I found myself constantly drained. After a while I started to notice that it was easier to follow the captions. Then I noticed that I was no longer "skimming" the school reading assignments. I was actually reading the assignments, and they were starting to make sense. Next thing I knew I was reading more than closed captions for pleasure, on top of school reading. Before I knew it, I had a PhD; not bad for having only read two books in high school.

My disability turned my weakness into a strength and leveraged it to achieve PTS. How incredible is that? As we read in chapter three, I used my disability to build a platform, without even realizing it. Now I have a personal library with thousands of books in it that I have read, and who'd have thought, I am even writing a book, and maybe someone will read it.

Resilience was instrumental to achieving PTS in my situation. Some people, such as the Ranger turned heroin addict, have a harder time bouncing back and finding a purpose. Thankfully I do not suffer from chronic pain as a side effect of my injuries. I have said it before and I will say it again, awareness of our choices is the key difference in whether you decide to be a disabled leader or a Disabled Leader.

Resilience should be a fundamental aspect of any recovery. Whether the person is struggling or not, everyone benefits from resilience awareness. Medical institutions focus on physically healing the patient as quickly as possible to free up the hospital bed, organizations want their employee back at work, families hope to put the tragedy behind them, and many times the disabled find themselves fighting for the future alone. Fighting for something more than survival. Figuring out how they can still accomplish all of their hopes and dreams. I hope that the medical professionals, family, and friends reading these words will recognize their Disabled Leaders potential and encourage resilience every day.

Share Your Disability Placard

In the last chapter I told you that you must never quit. Yet, now, here I am trying to figure out how to quit writing. I don't want to quit. I wish that I were a better writer, and could keep this book going for another two hundred pages. I am afraid that I am not clever or smart enough to hold your attention for that long. However, I hope that my readers realize that this is not the end, but the beginning.

If I have learned anything in the past ten years of teaching leadership, it is that every person who read this book is taking away something different. Even if it's from the same concept and the same paragraph, we each interpret the information differently. Not only am I ok with that, I encourage it. That is how we will expand and promote Disabled Leadership; by making it our own.

If you have read this far, my only request of you is to please take something away. Find something in here that can be useful to you. While I appreciate you reading these words, action is more important. Disabled Leaders make use of every resource available.

In all of my courses, the last class that I teach is Learning Transfer. I ask the students the same things that I am asking you *what is useful, how can you use it, and where will you begin?* Understanding learning transfer is important for achieving results. It's easy to read a book or go through a leadership course and then call yourself a leader. However, if you haven't changed or are not making plans to change, then how can you call yourself a leader?

Learning transfer refers to taking a concept from the classroom, or in this case, a book, and figuring out how to apply it in the operational environment (the real world). Chances are that the concept will look and feel much different when applied than it looks in our head. It will take dedication and discipline to create a tangible change.

We know the saying *the road to hell is paved with good intentions.* I have no doubt that you intend to be the best leader you can be, and may even use some of the theories you have learned here. I also know that it will be difficult. There will be challenges and opportunities. In the context of learning transfer, we call these barriers and interventions (opportunities).

Look, I know the idea of calling this leadership theory **D**isabled **L**eadership is a bit kooky. Many people will not be able to get past the title. So, when you start trying to convince people of the value, it may be difficult. Its, what I would call, a natural barrier. The same could be said for almost every topic covered in this book, or any leadership book. There will always be a naysayer. I can visualize you right now encouraging someone to break down their strengths and weaknesses and them scoffing and calling it a waste of time. We can't let these people deter us from our goals. If we accept something that they do not, that is ok. **D**isabled **L**eaders do not concern themselves with negative opinions.

The good news is that for every barrier that we face, we will find an opportunity. We have countless opportunities every day to change and develop. We also have more options with opportunities. Remember way back in the beginning of this book when I kept rambling about taking opportunities and making opportunities? Ah ha see I didn't forget. Opportunities present themselves every day, we just have to be willing to take them. The opportunities that don't present themselves are even more fun because we get to make those. Making opportunities may give us more control of the process. Making opportunities is certainly more empowering.

As you figure out what you want to use and where you want to start, I encourage flexibility, but I understand that some **D**isabled **L**eaders appreciate structure. A gentle reminder of what is valuable to you, what your goals are, and how you hope to achieve them. On the next page I have created and provided a **D**isabled **L**eader Development plan for you. No one will ever see it besides you, unless you choose to share it. At minimum, this may be a good time and place for you to write down any notes that you believe will be beneficial in helping you to succeed with your desired development.

Disabled Leader Development Plan

My key take-a-ways from Disabled Leadership are:

1. _____

2. _____

3. _____

Strengths Identified:

_____

Weaknesses Identified:

_____

Strategy Development:

Goals:

_____

What (Actions):

_____

Who (Key People):

_____

When (Suspense):

_____

Success Criteria:

_____

Why is this important:

_____

Opportunities:

_____

Barriers:

_____

Now you have a real and tangible plan. Keep it close. Put it somewhere that you will be forced to see it regularly. Most importantly, stick to the plan, even if you have to change it, keep moving. If you need too, make copies of the plan for additional goals.

We have a saying in Ranger Battalion: Slow is smooth, smooth is fast, and fast is deadly. The more politically correct way of saying that would be: go slow to go fast. That means don't try to change every aspect of your being overnight, don't try to save your organization in a week, and please do not tell your spouse that you can fix her. That is not the intent of **D**isabled **L**eadership. We have to start with ourselves. It sounds cliché but be the change that you want to see. Pick that one thing that you would like to see change and start there. Now, that doesn't mean if you want to improve your feedback giving abilities, that you should go office to office offering everyone feedback this week. Maybe start with asking for feedback more often. People will notice the change. *Hey did that weirdo Tom ask you for feedback after the meeting/project? Yeah, but I was actually glad that he did because I had some thoughts, but I didn't feel like the meeting was the appropriate time.* Just like that you have planted a seed for change. By modeling the behaviors that we believe drive **D**isabled **L**eadership, we are influencing others to change too. Remember, someone is always watching or listening.

As we have learned **D**isabled **L**eadership is about the choices we make. Do I choose to accept things as they are? Do I choose to accept defeat? Do I choose to fight? Do I choose to change? For each of those choices there are a million smaller, yet equally important, choices we will have to make. The road is long and hard, but there is a path, if we choose competence.

Noel Burch designed the four stages of competence.

Stage One: Unconscious Incompetence

Stage Two: Conscious Incompetence

Stage Three: Conscious Competence

Stage Four: Unconscious Competence

I enjoy this model for two reasons: 1. It is based on individual choice and 2. I get to call my students unconsciously incompetent. I'm not calling them stupid, but they don't know what they don't know. Just as you might not have guessed, when you first picked up this book, that **D**isabled **L**eadership might be a good thing. Still, you opened the book and perhaps read the abstract or skimmed over some of the pages. Most likely you thought, *hmmm I have never seen some of this before, it seems kind of crazy.* At that point you had reached stage two and became consciously incompetent. You became aware of a new (to you) concept. disabled leaders have a tough time accepting that there are things that they don't know.

May as well, you thought, *after all, it's on sale,* and you bought **D**isabled **L**eadership. Now here we are, at the end. You have read **D**isabled **L**eadership. You know what the theory demands and what it encourages. You have achieved stage three and are consciously competent. You know what "right" looks like. So, you have another decision to make. It's a big one. Do you buy in to **D**isabled **L**eadership? Buying in to Disabled Leadership is far harder than buying it. Do you want to try any of these approaches to life or business? Do you want to achieve stage four, unconscious competence? When you are unconsciously competent you exhibit **D**isabled **L**eadership traits without even thinking about it, it becomes second nature. It's your choice, no one can make it for you.

That may have been tough to follow; choices, stages of competence, what? Let me simplify the concept. Basically, all baby boomers, most Gen X, and many Gen Y readers had to learn how to drive a stick shift before their parents would allow them to drive an automatic. There rest of you will just have to take my word for it, a stick shift allows the driver to manually shift gears to go faster or slower.

We had been watching our parents drive for fifteen years, dreaming of this day. We are ready to rock, we got this. We get behind the wheel, crank the car, put it in first gear, and what happens next? Sputter, sputter, and stall. Why? We have been watching someone else do it for as long as we can remember, it should be easy. Just seeing someone else drive isn't enough. We were unconsciously incompetent. We had no idea how sensitive the clutch was. Now we are consciously incompetent. We understand there are a lot of moving pieces that we will have to master to become a competent driver.

So now we have a choice to make. Either we can put in the time and effort to learning how to shift through those gears, while still obeying traffic laws, or we can beg mom to take us to the mall on the weekends and maybe even to prom. That choice is easier for some than others. After a couple of dozen stall outs, we start to get the feel for the car. Now we can shift all the way through third gear without much issue. We are consciously competent. We know what right looks and feels like.

For the driver, making the step to the last stage is a no brainer. They have already put in the real work into figuring out how to shift properly, now they just need as much practice as possible to become unconsciously competent. It's not so simple for leaders, it is stacked up oppositely. The easy part is behind us. We know what right looks and feels like, but practicing it in "traffic" can be much scarier.

Ultimately the choice is yours. No one can force you to become a **D**isabled **L**eader, but remember, no one is forcing you to be a disabled leader either.

My hope is that we have created many new **D**isabled **L**eaders in the process of this journey. The majority of you were already **D**isabled **L**eaders, but you just didn't realize it. Many of you just needed a reminder of who you are and what you are about. Some of you know disabled leaders and I hope that you found something useful here to help influence them. Perhaps even some of you have realized that you've been exhibiting traits of a disabled leader; that's ok too.

This stuff isn't a secret. Sometimes I feel like if I have read one leadership book, I have read them all. Foundational leadership tactics simply get repackaged and presented in different ways. I obviously did not create a lot of this content, but I made sense of it in a different way. Hopefully a simpler way, that may reach a different demographic using a different lens.

In my experience interacting with thousands of disabled people throughout the years, I have never seen or heard anyone say that my disability is worse than yours. I have never heard anyone imply that their disability is better than another either. It would be weird if disabilities were a competition. Leadership is not a competition either. Disabled Leadership is not a leadership style, it is a philosophy, a way of life. It is not for everyone, but it can be for anyone.

This is not the end, but the beginning. Use the concepts in this book to build your own brand of Disabled Leadership. Try some these tools out for yourself. Go do more research on whatever topic intrigues you, and then try it. Make a little progress every day, starting today.

Acknowledgements

I would like to thank everyone who has bought, read, and shared Disabled Leadership for their ongoing support. It takes everyone to change a culture. Although he has passed on, I thank Delford Smith for providing me with leadership opportunities which have helped me soar and continue to shoot for the stars. I thank everyone that I have taught with and learned from at the US Army during my career, you have helped me refine my understanding of leadership. Most importantly, I thank Colleen Papendieck for tolerating my stubbornness, finally convincing me that I cannot edit my own work, and assisting me with final revisions. Without this team, this book and indeed theory, would not be possible.

Citations

1. Jensen, E. (2009). *Teaching with poverty in mind: What being poor does to kids' brains and what schools can do about it*. AScD.

2. Maxwell, J. C. (2013). Everything rises and falls on leadership.

3. Uhl-Bien, M., Marion, R., & McKelvey, B. (2007). Complexity leadership theory: Shifting leadership from the industrial age to the knowledge era. *The leadership quarterly*, *18*(4), 298-318.

4. Zieziula, F. (1998). The world of the deaf community. *Living with grief: Who we are, how we grieve, 181198*.

5. Freeman Jr, S., & Kochan, F. (2019). Exploring mentoring across gender, race, and generation in higher education: An ethnographic study. *International Journal of Mentoring and Coaching in Education*.

6. Merryman, A. (2013). Losing is good for you. *New York Times*.

7. Sauer, S. J., Thomas-Hunt, M. C., & Morris, P. A. (2010). Too good to be true? The unintended signaling effects of educational prestige on external expectations of team performance. *Organization Science*, *21*(5), 1108-1120.

8. Greene, D. (2002). *Fight your fear and win: Seven skills for performing your best under pressure--at work, in sports, on stage*. Harmony.

9. Moscovitch, D. A., Gavric, D. L., Senn, J. M., Santesso, D. L., Miskovic, V., Schmidt, L. A., ... & Antony, M. M. (2012). Changes in judgment biases and use of emotion regulation strategies during cognitive-behavioral therapy for social anxiety disorder: distinguishing treatment responders from nonresponders. *Cognitive Therapy and Research*, *36*(4), 261-271.

10. Rimal, R. N., & Real, K. (2005). How behaviors are influenced by perceived norms: A test of the theory of normative social behavior. *Communication research*, *32*(3), 389-414.

11. Robertson, K. (2005). Active listening: more than just paying attention. *Australian family physician*, *34*(12), 1053.

12. Tugend, A. (2008). Multitasking can make you lose... um... focus. *The New York Times*, *24*.

13. Mumby, D. K. (2007). Organizational communication. *The Blackwell encyclopedia of sociology*.

14. Andreasen, N. C. (2011). What is post-traumatic stress disorder?. *Dialogues in clinical neuroscience*, *13*(3), 240.

15. Collins, J. (2009). Good to Great-(Why Some Companies Make the Leap and others Don't).

16. Uslaner, E. M. (1999). Trust but verify: Social capital and moral behavior. *Social Science Information*, *38*(1), 29-55.

17. Rempel, J. K., Holmes, J. G., & Zanna, M. P. (1985). Trust in close relationships. *Journal of personality and social psychology*, *49*(1), 95.

18. Madsen, P. M., & Desai, V. (2010). Failing to learn? The effects of failure and success on organizational learning in the global orbital launch vehicle industry. *Academy of Management Journal, 53*(3), 451-476.

19. Ross, R. (1994). The ladder of inference. *The fifth discipline fieldbook: Strategies and tools for building a learning organization*, 242-246.

20. Valkenburg, R. C. (1998). Shared understanding as a condition for team design. *Automation in construction, 7*(2-3), 111-121.

21. Wilkinson, A. (1998). Empowerment: theory and practice. *Personnel review, 27*(1), 40-56.

22. Luhmann, N. (2018). *Trust and power*. John Wiley & Sons.

23. Colby, A., James, J. B., & Hart, D. (Eds.). (1998). *Competence and character through life* (pp. 89-112). Chicago, IL: University of Chicago Press.

24. Hart, G. (1996). The five W's: An old tool for the new task of task analysis. *Technical communication, 43*(2), 139-145.

25. Sinek, S. (2009). *Start with why: How great leaders inspire everyone to take action*. Penguin.

26. Ancker, C. J. (2013). The evolution of mission command 4 in US Army Doctrine, 1905 to the present. *Military review, 93*(2), 42.

27. De Brabandere, L., & Iny, A. (2013). *Thinking in new boxes: A new paradigm for business creativity*. Random House Incorporated.

28. De Bono, E. (2017). *Six thinking hats*. Penguin UK.

29. Elder, L., & Paul, R. (2007). Universal intellectual standards. *Foundation for Critical Thinking*.

30. Thomas, K. W. (2008). Thomas-Kilmann Conflict Mode.

31. Page, D., & Donelan, J. G. (2003). Team-building tools for students. *Journal of Education for Business, 78*(3), 125-128.

32. Chamberlain, J. L. (1994). *Bayonet! Forward: My Civil War Reminiscences*. Butternut & Blue.

33. Deci, E., & Ryan, R. M. (1985). *Intrinsic motivation and self-determination in human behavior*. Springer Science & Business Media.

34. Dichter, E. (2017). *The strategy of desire*. Routledge.

35. Brown, B. A., Emerson, T. I., Falk, G., & Freedman, A. E. (1970). The equal rights amendment: A constitutional basis for equal rights for women. *Yale Lj, 80*, 871.

36. Berg, R. K. (1964). Equal Employment Opportunity Under the Civil Rights Act of 1964. *Brook. L. Rev., 31*, 62.

37. Morin, E. C. (1990). Americans with Disabilities Act of 1990: Social integration through employment. *Cath. UL Rev., 40*, 189.

38. Kahn, R. (2015). Right to Same-Sex Marriage: Formalism, Realism, and Social Change in Lawrence (2003), Windsor (2013), and Obergefell (2015). *Md. L. Rev., 75*, 271.

39. Boyd, S. B. (2015). Equality: An uncomfortable fit in parenting law. *Equality: An Uncomfortable Fit in Parenting Law", in Robert Leckey, ed., After Legal Equality: Family, Sex, Kinship (Routledge 2015)*, 42-58.

40. Nalder, E., Hartman, L., Hunt, A., & King, G. (2018). Traumatic brain injury resiliency model: a conceptual model to guide rehabilitation research and practice. *Disability and rehabilitation*, 1-10.

Made in the USA
Columbia, SC
24 August 2022

65389742R00129